Howls from the Wolfpack

ISBN-10: 0615439063
EAN-13: 9780615439068

Howls from the Wolfpack

Acknowledgements from the Authors

Many thanks to Thorin for giving us this opportunity first off.

Then thanks to Randal, Ben, Da Nekidgoat, and RJ for the help putting this together, while writing their own sections. Thanks to RJ for thinking up the book's title, and to Swatcop for thinking up the name for the publishing company, Abyss Press.

Thanks to the many contributors to this project. Too many to list.

From us all, we would like to thank those friends and family who were behind us on this project.

Dedication

This book is dedicated to all of you. Whoever you are, if you have picked up this book and begun reading, then our writings are for you. The sheep that simply follow, we dedicated this to you to try and release you from your chains. For the black sheep that need to shed the last of your wool. And even for the wolves that need more fuel for the fire that is inside you. These words are ours, for each one of you.

Disclaimer

Thorin, Wicked Jester, Inc, Ronin, Abyss Press, or any of its affiliates do not endorse or sponsor any views expressed in this book. All views expressed are the sole view of the submitting author and of the submitting author alone. This book is merely a collection of ideas, insights, and thoughts of individuals with the wolf mentality. As any true wolf knows, we are each the exclusive authors of our own thoughts.

Table of Contents

CONTENTS

Introduction
Welcome to the Badlands

S peaking with a couple of the other writers in this book, one said he is already well known for his individuality and that put a target on his back. The other one said he likes targets and he's polishing his bulls-eye. Makes you think, isn't anyone who stands up and speaks their mind a target? For hate, and fear or admiration and inspiration. You have a classroom, and the teacher asks a question, do you see the whole class raise their hands? No, just a couple, the ones who will speak their mind. Easily distinguished from the rest, simply by the fact they spoke.

This book is our opportunity to speak up, and speak our minds, open our souls, take it or leave it. Different backgrounds and ages, all with the Think for yourself mentality that is the Wolf, yet still unique. Leaders of ourselves and followers of none. Unafraid to stand up when everyone else is going along to get along. This makes us targets on a bigger stage, and if you wish to challenge us on our thoughts, a few of us have websites, emails or go to www.stalkingtheflock.com and enter what Thorin calls the Badlands. Stand up to the challenge that is life. Open this book and step into a new world.

Ronin

The Mountain

By Thorin

A long the rocky faces of the lower foothills, a young wolf walks alone. He struggles and stumbles as he slowly transverses the terrain. As he ascends the foothills toward the mountain ahead, his path becomes blocked by a deep chasm. While standing along the chasm he instinctively howls down into the dark depths of the canyon below, "Why is it so?" After a brief moment, a chorus of voices echo back from the darkness, "Because it has always been." The young wolf ponders this answer for a few moments and then bellows back a stern, "Why?" Instead of a reply, the canyon simply goes silent. The young wolf stares at the wide gap in the earth's crust. As moments pass, the young wolf conjures some courage, digs his claws deep into the rocky surface and then in a single bound, leaps right over the deep chasm. Without looking back, the young wolf keeps stride and continues his journey with the mountain ahead locked squarely in his line of sight.

Many moons pass as the lone wolf continues to move closer and closer to the mountain. After he transverses many canyons and after passing through numerous fences, he ascends out of the foothills and reaches the lower region of the mountain itself.

As he approaches the base, he encounters a friendly man. The man, wearing a decorative cloak and carrying a finely crafted crooked staff, warns the young wolf of the dangers, pitfalls, and consequences of preceding any farther up the face of the treacherous mountain.

The man is full of advice which he freely offers to the young wolf. His fear inducing stories of what has happened to other wolves who have tried climbing past the point in which he now stands are very convincing. The man then offers the wolf a comfortable place to bed down and seems eager to teach the young canine many more lessons. The man speaks of the multitude of his friendly followers and how they would all love to meet and welcome him. He offers his acceptance of the wolf and asks that in return for his embrace he simply shaves his fur, and trims back his claws so that he can fit in with the rest of his group which are comfortably nestled down in the lush valley below.

As the wolf considers taking the nice man up on his offer, he decides that his personal goal of reaching the mountain's summit is more important. He feels that he has already come too far to back down now, so he politely thanks the man for his offer and then states that he must be heading on his way. Upon declining the offer, the man seems angered; his attitude changes almost instantaneously. He threatens the young wolf, "Stay here or you will be sorry. If you turn down my offer and refuse to join us, you will be forever shunned, ridiculed, and damned to spend the rest of your years alone!" The young wolf snarls back, "I'll take my chances". Then, with the flip of his tail, the young wolf dashes off into the dense brush leaving the man to himself.

Years pass as the wolf continues climbing toward the summit. By now the numerous challenges of the mountain have honed him; the years of his unrelenting persistence have tempered him; the pains of overcoming multitudes of adversities encountered along his chosen path have strengthened him. He now nears the summit as an older, wiser, and more enlightened being. For years he has endured the foothills, the badlands, the canyons, and many persuasive characters who have all attempted to break his sprit and stifle his goals. He has been alone on his mountainous path pushing forward with the support of no one but himself. Now, as he finally nears the summit, the sun begins to rise, and for the first time he watches the rays break over the last peak as they land warmly upon his face.

As he confidently walks the last few hundred yards to the pinnacle, he notices movement in the distance. To his astonishment, this lone wolf who has traveled in solitude for so many years sees tiny spots ahead starting to assemble. As he draws closer to them, the distant figures begin to howl in his direction. "What is this?" he thinks to himself. Then he realizes it is a pack of fellow wolves welcoming him to the mountain's summit!

He once thought that he was destined to forever roam alone. Along his path he finally came to the understanding that destiny is not assigned, but rather what one makes it. Upon his final ascent, he came to understand that there is no greater reward than that of just being true to one's self. Through his trials, tribulations, and rejections, he now gains the fellowship of a small, rare breed that is different in every way but one: they all remain true to themselves. He understands that it is always preferable to bear the pain of alienation for being who he is than to gain the praise of conditional acquaintances who accept him only at the cost of his own integrity and personal thoughts.

Although this wolf now claims his home at the mountain's summit alongside his kindred, he still descends down in the valley from time to time... not to visit, but to stalk and feed.

Alex Harber

Wicked Johnny

Meet the Pack

I'm just a man that has been placed on this earth and I will make most of this life. I have been put through hell and walked out bloody and burnt, but I survived. The majestic Phoenix must burn to become born again, and that's how I live my life. I have taken myself to a lower level than most in this world, and that has built me stronger. Forming myself into the negative one, I have created a being in myself that is stronger than I could have ever imagined, and I embrace that beast, the wolf I have become.

Echo

Burning alive,
Infernal fire,
Demon inside,
Rising higher.
Hell's pit,
Home ground,
Ever lost,
Never found.

We've survived,
Heaven and hell.
We're denying,
The world you sell.
Lock us up,
Throw away the key,
Fight till death,
That will be your fee.

Rusty chains,
Hold us down,
Blood spills,
Onto the crown,
Our hands,
Now are free,
The wolf's howl,
Echoes every scream.

KnuckleHead

I've been picked up and slammed back down.

Beat by my own and pushed to the ground.

No matter what I do I can never win.

Everything falls apart, away, and then

I stand back up shattered and bloody

I start to laugh so you ask, "What's so funny?"

"It's very simple," I say with a couple of chuckles

I'm taking back control with my knuckles!

Bullets

✦ If what does not kill us makes us stronger, what of that which does kill us?

✦ You see a God, while I see nothing more than a lowly shepherd.

✦ You look and laugh at me. It's sad you think the truth is funny.

𝔍𝔲𝔰𝔱 𝔯𝔢𝔞𝔡 𝔍𝔱.

.elbissop sa hcum sa dnatsrednu ot ,neewteb-ni dna kcab ,drawrof sdaer flow A .mottob ot pot ,thgir ot tfel ,nrettap lamron eht swollof peehs A .peehs a morf flow a llet ot yaw tsetsaf eht si gnidaeR

Most people that have read the words we have written will simply look at them for face value rather than understanding them for their core truths and lessons. To truly understand what we are saying you cannot just read the words. Anyone can look at a series of letters and repeat them, as though they are accepted truths. Only through discipline can one read words, internalize them, and see their true meanings, see what they are really saying.

Sheep read books that are revered by critics, and simply run their eyes past the words memorizing quotes they hear others say. They take the letters and add sounds to them, and spew them back out at any chance they get. They recite facts they read to sound smart, they recite philosophy to sound like they have experience. They use big words because they sound educated, but rarely do they understand that word, and others don't ask.

A wolf will take each word, put it to the grindstone and see what is the truth or lies behind it. We take each letter and not only add a sound to it but a specific meaning according to the context that letter is placed into. We are the ones that are able to take something that uses educated speech and simplify it, so it is easier to understand, because we understand it. We quote philosophy, not because we cannot think of what to say, but because we realize that, sometimes, someone else has already said it best, and we can apply that philosophy to the world, and the situation.

There are many ways to read, and even more to understand. You will not learn the same as I, nor the same as anyone else. So ask yourself a simple question, are you simply reading the words or are you understanding these howls?

Benjamin K. Adams

Cazut_Arhangel

Meet The Pack

I am the one known as Cazut Arhanghel. I am the fallen angel to those I am around. I am the silent shadow that can be seen at winter's daybreak. I am of the Old Knight's Code. I uphold this with honor and respect. I am an US Army Veteran and I will fight. I am of two minds within one body. I am proud to hold both Germany and Ireland in my blood. I will never fight but I will always defend. I will not hesitate to take the life of another but will show mercy. I challenge society as a whole and have won each duel. I am forged under the fires of war and hatred to rise above as the tactician of the Light. I surpass your Time and see beyond the veil. You are a pawn to my knight. I will come at you with great vengeance from out beyond. I am the Devil's Advocate in your society. Challenge me and you will fight. Challenge me and you may fall. I am insane but I am sound.

Hate The Wolf; Love The Sheep

You, ye who judges from within the flock
You see me through narrow eyes perched on a scornful look
I tell you now, don't hate me based on your ignorance
If you're going to hate me then hate me for this
Hate me because I am different
Hate me because I can stand on my own two feet
Hate me because I am smart with common sense
Hate me because I am intelligent
Hate me because I can defend against you
Don't you dare hate me because of your own selfish reasons or gains
Don't hate me because I can see through you
Don't hate me because you are weak

Love your own kind you coward among ants
Love those you see as a mirror of your own self
Oh how you praise those who stand as you scorn those same in the delusional privacy you have
You sheep love this box paradox
I am hated for I have burnt mine in front of your very eyes
I delight in your hatred for it fuels my existence; my sanity and my love to grow
Let winter be time of your judgment
For I will stalk your flock within the shadows you fear and cover with those of the flock's

I testify against you
I plead you hate me
I ask I be hated for I hold truth
I urge you to hate me because truth is in my heart
I am on my knees begging you despise my existence
As existence that will never assimilate
I say finally to you, who is ready for shearing and fattening, Love me for these two reasons

Love me because I have an extra set of fangs for your muzzle
Love me because I can break your hooves into claws

Bullets

✦ The hunt isn't over until both your heart and your belly are full.

✦ The question is never who or what, but is more why and how.

Social Darwinism's Truth

Abstract

A fairly old concept, Social Darwinism is constantly looked at in new light. But in long standing, Charles Darwin discovered his views on adaptation within a species after Herbert Spencer created his views and theories for survival of the fittest. This country seems to understand the concepts of only the strongest will survive and cannot dictate a proper balance between survival with equality and freedom. The theory of only the strongest stands strong through the test of time but of course is unfathomable when used to its max potential due to today's standards of ethics. With so many Government programs, in today's society the weakest have found a way to thrive and live as if rich without effort or a work-discipline. Free hand-outs have allowed for the weak to thrive and have dismantled natural law within society by providing a crutch.

Social Darwinism's Truth

In a society of quicksand where handouts are as numerous as the grain of sand on a beach are, the fostering of strength and the worth to fight has become diminishing. With several government aid programs to help the so called needy society has lost the value of an earned dollar. Instead, society will foster the weak under a warm blanket and feed them food paid for by those who break their backs this is the safety provided for. But what safety is there to for? What danger does denial hinder seeing? The ironclad fist has begun to pound at the ground from the strikes of the mighty. Although the strongest will survive any society-like hierarchy, it is the elite's role to provide tools that will allow the weakest to grow and thrive without prolonged support.

Survival of the fittest, a natural law befitted to all animals, including the species known as man. The definition of Social

BENJAMIN K. ADAMS (CAZUT_ARHANGEL)

Darwinism speaks about those who are strong will grow in power and in cultural influence over the weak. The strongest should flourish in society. The weak and unfit should be allowed to die. The weak were to diminish and their culture delimited. One philosopher chiefly expounded the theory and obtained boost of application through Darwin's ideas such as adaptation and survival of the fittest.

The philosophy's views and elitist thoughts like "Might is right" were in long standing prior to the published works of Charles Darwin. With these points created by Darwin, the philosopher was able to justify his ethical theory on a more nature-based level. Adaptation and natural selection were two prominent ideals that showed the majority of Social Darwinism's justification. The concept of adaptation was used to prove the positions of the rich and powerful were people who were better adapted to the social and economic climate of their time. On a nature paralleled view natural selection allowed the philosopher to argue his theory as natural, normal, and proper for the strong to thrive at the expense of the weak.

As with any social theory, whether it is Socialism, Communism, Capitalism or Social Darwinism, it is designed solely for the use of economic prosperity at the highest level. However, there are other aspects to this prosperity. One point to prosperity is colonialism. This aspect involves the subjugation of one people to another. Two examples of colonialism have been used to justify ethics within Social Darwinism. The first is the involvement of the British colonialism in India which was defended by Karl Marx. The second is local Americans driving the Native Americans from their lands. Colonialism is nothing new, Greeks, Romans and the Ottomans are only a few of many old cultures who have used this form of territorial expansion.

A second application of Social Darwinism is its most extreme form. Because of the echoing lines of "might is right" and survival of the fittest, justifications have been set up towards eugenics programs that were aimed at removing undesirable genes within a population. Such programs were sometimes accompanied by sterilization laws directed at *unfit* individuals.

Not all of Social Darwinism can be accredited in a negative view. Some followers used their high status or place among the *fittest* to provide resources to aid the weak into becoming strong. The belief in this theory discouraged wanton handouts to the poor, favoring instead to provide resources for the fittest of all walks of life. Some combined philanthropy with Social Darwinism and created numerous libraries and public institutions, for the benefit of those who would choose to avail themselves with such resources.

Within society people have an unknown identity they carry with them like the shirts on their backs. Many people believe they know who they are and will associate themselves with a political alliance, or a group or an organization. Nevertheless, what these people don't understand is that their mentality has its own identity. For people have come to realize just what this identity is. People like Thorin and others have published works, which expands on this mentality. In their works, the analogies of wolves, sheep and sheepdogs are highly focused.

Each animal analogy represents a certain group mentality that is centered on the individual. Sheep mentality, also known as herd mentality, is a person, who at the highest level, lives in denial. Denial of violence, bad things happening to THEM, while wanting "safety nets."

A wolf in popular view is a person who has the capacity for violence and has no empathy for fellow citizen. In other words, a wolf in society is a well-defined aggressive sociopath. The difference which makes the sheepdog different from a wolf is the sense of empathy. This idea proves helpful for identifying why a person can perform duties of any military branch, local fire department or any area within the police department.

Very similar to other's thoughts, Thorin made a similar observation. In all of Thorin's books the use of sheep and wolves is designed to separate the mass majority and the lesser minority.

He does not use the term sheepdog in his writings; however, he uses the image of a wolf as a warrior. The relation between Thorin's sheep and wolves is the concept of yin-yang with only one difference. Within the symbol of yin-yang there are small circles of the opposite color. This shows equality in everything, there is strength in weakness; there is weakness in strength. The difference is sheep construct the yin, they are weak and passive. Yang creates the wolf, an active, expanding, and strong being. But what makes the difference is yang does not possess the smaller opposite colored circle. This entails sheep have the capacity to become wolves but wolves do not have the capacity to become sheep. This is evolution.

Like the self-reliant's concept of sheep, Thorin's definition does not change. Sheep are creatures that deny the existence of the wolf. They are an ignorant race of man who lacks taking the initiative. In the eyes of Thorin, this is the reason to evolve into a wolf. A wolf is a being of his or her own design. The wolf is the one who will take what is provided and what is presented and bash it into something tender through the use of reasoning in the form of a filter. Thorin best described a wolf in his book *The Wolf in Wolf's Clothing*, "I do not succumb to peer pressure, for I possess will...I am completely unfettered, unrestricted, and untrained...mentally unchained. I am negatively positive... perfectly flawed" (Thorin, p. 29, 2008)

The concepts Social Darwinism uses from Darwin are naturalistic in theory. But there is more to the basic views of survival of the fittest within mankind. There are actual gears working in the lives of those who live by this view. One author posited that man removing from himself everything and reverting back to a more primitive state. In this state there will be no law but only the laws of nature. discrediting the politician's use of laws and traditions as well as political standards-of-value and dogmas, that the law of the land that is laid down by man's hands. Returning to the wild, back to Nature for moral standards. And that each searches their own hearts for the meaning of right and wrong.

This law is nothing new. The reflection of the words show the events that lead to present day are of survival of only the strongest. And the strongest got to that level by sheer will power, letting nothing stop them. From here, we can see another gear that turns the Social Darwinist wheel. This is also what divides sheep from wolves, the weak from the strong.

It is might that pushes the strong upward towards the sky and allow them to rise above all. But it is also the same theory or life style that promotes to provide the sheep a possible way to evolve and become wolves so that they can claim a place for themselves with other warriors of strength.

It is the duty to excel the race as a whole by providing to strengthen another's weakness. This is mandated by Nature itself towards a species that is socially based. The exclusion of government aid and the addition of government resources for skill refinement or obtainment will better fit the theory of the fittest survival. In a community where equality must be tolerated, instead take only what is given, you get treated as you treat others.

Conformity, The Slowest Form Of Suicide

As we walk through our educational lives, we form bonds and relationships with those around us we can relate to. Elementary school gives us the chance to become a part of something that is larger than our own self. We make bonds and meet new people that we later on are able to relate to. In Junior High School, we start to create groups of people we become welcomed and accepted by. This group of people we claim as friends to ourselves and who we can fall back on for help. But as we progress to High School, these groups segregate from everyone. They come to grow against popular belief, a certain view point, certain activities and they come to grow against or around many factors. But there is a specific group, a specific clique that goes against the norm. This group refuses to uphold the rights and wrongs of the surrounding society and who stand against the popular beliefs. This group defines hardcore. They stand against the current that is guided and steered by the society in which they live with. These individuals will walk, run, and beat their way against any pressure or force that stands to make all the same. That is why I believe non-conformity is the better way of life than wanting to fit into a group of people who, as a whole, restrain the person's personal being and removes any hint of difference.

With my history of hard work, dedication and strong resolve to finish my tasks as well as my increasing will to help all those I can who are around me. I was a very kind-hearted individual who just did what was asked of me and did not question the motives or the reasons. My grades demonstrated motivation within the subject but also would show that I was challenged for they did not stick to high grades and would rather fluctuate from the extremes on the grading system. My participation was highly valued whereas my speech was quite weak since I barely spoke aloud and I let my actions show my own emotions and views for the most part. But this is all through Junior High School. Things change significantly within the first year of Senior High School. Of my nature to speak through my actions and to work on something that is worth doing right (i.e.: school projects; homework assignments, etc), I had a difficult time with much bullying that occurred through each and every day. I, being labeled a geek, a nerd, weakling and numerous other degrading terms, could not "fit in" into any sort of group that existed or was present. I faced many views and thoughts that went against my own. That is until I decided to look around the school at each student individually. Then I noticed each difference and the similarities I had with them. So I chose the group of people I will have strength with. They are called band-geeks.

Everyone may relate to several groups in a school but will only be labeled and take on the name of just one group. Band-geeks are different. We take on around 3 names for ourselves at most. We let our intelligence and our innovation take the lead part of our lives and we stick out among our fellow students proudly. We do not stand with or against those around us. We live by our own codes of sticking together and helping one another to improve on musical skill and have each other think from outside the box on the day's current issues, which improved the intelligence of the group as a whole.

Through the four years of the public schooling, I have grown stronger and have been able to withstand the current of the stream. But with such I have faced many oppositions. I have endured numerous threats of physical harm. These never declined due to my nature of silence and the complacency of the surrounding faculty within the school system. But shortly after the start of these threats I noticed these bullies could not keep their word. I soon developed a simple notion and a small motto-like thought. I could give the motto but a still-favorite author of that time has a better, well put and simplified saying. Thorin states this in his writings, "I don't issue ideal threats I give sincere predictions." These threats were due to my inability to conform to the views and ideals of those around me. I would not back down from my own views for I knew they were truth and have not been proven against to make them deemed wrong. These threats also had a more physical based reason. Since the school favored its sports and those who participate within the teams, those a part of the teams are given a status that exempts them from equal punishment as those who are not a part of the sports programs. Because I would not participate in a sport all the jocks would focus their selves on us who take no part or assimilation to sports. But an interesting concept came to light; the strength of an individual can be brought down by the quick wittedness of another. Because of my already high intellect, higher than the average High School student, I decided to switch focuses and aim to their weaknesses. My energy and time went to learning outside the school facility and have given me mental scars and lessons that one shouldn't learn at such a young age. But the confidence rose and rose and rose. Where I immediately challenged all those who threaten me proving them cowards who cannot keep any word they promise. Thorin once said in his previously published book, "Education is the most effective form of rebellion." Where sports team members focus on brute force and physical stamina I did the same in studies and knowledge not found in the school. But my rebellion here is against the school's injustice.

Through all of High School, I have faced much opposition. Through all of High School I have dealt with a lot of ignorance. Through all of High School, I have been surrounded by numerous individuals who have a herd-like mentality. I walked the halls as if I was the only light in a room of darkness. Being evident, oppression had become a main problem in my life. Because I wanted to live as I know how, those around me thought differently. They all believed everyone should be the same and should achieve at the same rate, or least have similar goals to achieve since we were took the exact classes as anyone one else. But this was a different matter for me. I wanted to strive in a secluded setting, meaning I didn't want the influence of those around me to guide my thoughts so to speak. I wanted to imitate the learning so many famous scientists before me have experienced. I wanted to start with nothing but a book and excel to know the contents by heart and have the abilities to demonstrate the knowledge. But because of the socializing that occurs inevitably, I could not grasp the whole goal in the end. But as in everything else, there are loop-holes. This loop-hole to allow my growth came from the timing of everyone's personal schedule. My rebellion was to arrive to a destination everyone around me deemed unwanted in disgust.

With the use of Toulmin's graph, I can now see more clearly what my claims, reasons, warrants and my values and beliefs are that motivate my personal being through such times as High School, College and life for that matter. The one claim that I want to make clear and is also evident is the act of independency. Because conformity requires assimilation and for you to be similar to those around you, the individual aspect of one's life is completely eroded away with the factors of time and peer pressure. I learned a simple rule when all this was nearing the end of High School. I learned that not everything will always be good or bad; positive or negative. I learned that everything in itself has both positive and negative consequences. No matter what I was to do or what another was to do against or for me, I would always reap the goods of something positive as well as negative. Therefore, my rebellion against the conforming structure and body of the society around me can be worded best as such: "Adversity is like a flame, it melts the weak but it tempers the strong."

As I have said in the story, my reasons are themselves. I first faced opposition. Opposition works against us like water wearing down the earth. It breaks us down to our most basic and most influential state of being. It is the influential state that starts our path to becoming everyone else or to harden and become who we are. I faced opposition from every student I encountered. But I was not influenced to follow their path but instead secluded myself to grow and refine myself. Just as if I was metal to a blacksmith's hammer I re-forged my own being to rise above the people around me.

The societal views of those who strive to become themselves and to achieve personal are biased. Society yearns to have its communities excel and become stronger. But the bias of these views only applies to when an individual of the community strives to reach the goal without the influence or guide of the society. Rules and guidelines are put into action when these people are able to stand against the opposition and scrutiny of the other people. The rules and guidelines are used to tear down the resources used by the individuals and to limit them on their success. The more opportunities taken away from these people the more strife they will be in conflict with.

Next and final are the values and beliefs that I uphold through this story. These concepts are very strong in it themselves. They are thoughts that can push one to realize their own potential in life. I have used a few of these in the story itself. They are the quotes I have used from a few books by the author Thorin. These quotes again are: "Adversity is like a flame, it melts the weak but it tempers the strong", "Education is the most effective form of rebellion". Another belief that I mentioned on briefly, though indirectly is this: "When injustice becomes law, Rebellion becomes duty." These are all the beliefs I had gathered and came to terms with. But a value that I have stated numerous times is the act of rebellion. In my story I use rebellion as my own personalized voice. Because my speech is weak and I speak clearly through my actions, a rebellion is the same as a verbal protest. A protest that I can become something better more refined without the use or distractions of influential thoughts.

In summary, the best things that you can ever gain are the rewards of hardship of opposition, peer pressure and the society itself working against you. But the rewards reaped are sweeter than honey and allows more doors of opportunities because your skills would be finer and more focused. That is in due to the excelling mind to go further into a subject of skill and to grasp more at a time than when taught to progress with those around you. However, to finalize my thoughts I have learned to give back to those who suppress me equal to what I receive from them. "Hate for Hate and Ruth for Ruth, Eye for Eye and Tooth for Tooth, Scorn for Scorn and Smile for Smile, Love for Love and Guile for Guile, War for War and Woe for Woe, Blood for Blood and Blow for Blow."

The Tale Of The Panicked King

In the recently published book, *The Wolf in Wolf's Clothing 2nd Edition* by Thorin, He takes a side tangent and writes a satirical 'interlude'. The title of the fictional story is *Pan and the King.* The story begins with a king worrying about his kingdom when morale and support within the kingdom began to fall into dreadfully low states. As with any king of a region, when a king is unable to perform an act on his own he must turn to religion and rituals for guidance and wisdom in order to fix a perilous situation. The king turns towards summoning the great god Pan (the Greek god of shepherds and flocks). After several attempts and having no success, the court was dismissed and the king is left in solitude sitting on his throne. The king takes a bottle of wine and consumes it that very night as he drifts speaking "If I only had more control......"(Thorin, 60). He wakes to a sense of apathy and saw Pan standing before him. Pan pointed out a book sitting upon the king's lap and the king was unable to open the book. Pan made the observation that the king's heart is in the wrong place. Thereafter Pan spoke in an unknown language and summoned two different kings who were then shown to be the present king's predecessors. One king ruled with persuasion while the other king ruled with an iron fist.

The majority of the pages that followed were filled with the two kings arguing with each other that their way was more superior to ruling a kingdom. However, with each statement pronounced, the opposite king would then reveal its flaw. When the argument came to a halt, Pan spoke saying, "both kings are only half right, as they are also half wrong" (Thorin, 63). "Gain foothold with the quill, maintain posture with the sword" (Thorin, 63), this is the lesson to be learned by the king through Pan's actions. After the king absorbed Pan's wisdom, the king tried opening the book on his lap once more, and this time is successful he flips through its bindings to read the words "...

His reign lasted very long, and even today, his actions echo throughout the ages" (Thorin, 64).

How can such a short story contain so much information? At first glance of the text, you will know it is a king in trouble who seeks aid and guidance from beyond the realm of man. He is answered, only after becoming disoriented, by the great god Pan. Pan shows him two paths by which the king may rule and tosses the king a curve ball by saying both are only half-right while they are also half wrong. This lesson shows that the king must find a harmonious mixture between the two paths to rule his kingdom for a long period of time. But there is much more behind the story than this simple lesson.

On observation of the text, you come to realize the entire story is a metaphor for herding a flock of sheep. Because of this metaphor it will make the king himself the shepherd, the kingdom's citizens the sheep and the kingdom the pasture, and respectably the wolves as the kingdom's enemies. How perfect is it to use the Greek god of shepherds and flocks to aid a king to regain back his falling kingdom? What other story(s) is like this? What can be better than to be given a riddle that shows two sides to a king questioning himself? The two sides given by the god of shepherds and flocks are the end points of the ruling style spectrum. Rule by persuasion and reap loyalty and respect is one king's path. The opposite king's path is to rule on a kingdom built on blood and bone.

The basis of the argument between the two kings, Retrac and Hsub, is that it is pointless to rule by word that is void of action and it is pointless if to rule solely by ruthless actions devoid of reason. King Retrac ruled long with persuasion, building trust and giving respect. He made each man an equal and ruled with honor. "You cannot rule with a scepter when your sword is two-handed" (Thorin, 62). Whereas King Hsub ruled on blood and bone, "The best kings are not those who talk weak, but those who act strong" (Thorin, 61). Throughout this argument, something odd happens, as with an argument two people pose opposite sides and never agree to the opposition, in this argument both kings constantly agree with one another before they discredit with the reality of positions. One example is when King Hsub states that you must lay opposition to rest because the effects of misinformation will always trump what's best (Thorin, 62). King Retrac then states he agrees with the statement but soon says it is better to be a leader of equals than a king of fools (Thorin, 63).

The problem trying to be fixed in the story is a common problem in our lives. When the story is finished, the king opens the book where the last lines are read as the ending of the story. When Pan awakens the young king, he has a book placed on top of the king's lap. The king's ability to open the book is the test in which to find the root of the problem. With the king's failure to open the book evident, Pan laughs abruptly and states that the problem is obvious (Thorin, 61). The king learns that his heart is in the wrong place. When Pan summons two kings equal in difference in looks and ruling positions, Pan makes it apparent to the king that his heart and his desires are disconnected. The king learns from the wisdom provided by the two summoned kings. Unlike giving words of counsel that many kings would seek, Pan steers off and presents the extremes of two possible answers or solutions to regaining back the morale and support of his kingdom. With this way of giving the king wisdom and advice, the young king is able to observe two different physical realities. By learning this way, the young king can come to a realization of two possible futures for himself rather than to reflect upon words and create much error during his ruling in the kingdom. This is a common problem we have in our lives, what Pan does is the necessary action we should take. Instead of viewing the problem and all the flaws it exposes, we should instead look at the relationship the acclaimed problem has with ourselves.

Works Cited

Thorin (2007-2008)."Pan and the King". The Wolf in Wolf's Clothing. *Wicked Jester Inc.* pp. 58-64.

Burke

My Steps From Wool To Fur

I think I was born with at least a Black Sheep Mentality or Wolf Mentality but it still took me a while to fully shed my wool and become a Wolf. When I was young I was very sick and in the hospital a lot and almost died one time from Chicken Pox and Scarlet Fever together so from a very early age I was fighting for my very existence. And now my view is that the world tried to take me out at an early age and failed so "good luck with that" now cause I won't go quietly. Even in school I had the Wolf Mentality just didn't have a label for it then. I can remember being thrown out of classes because I questioned the teacher on things that didn't sound right to me. I didn't do it to disrupt class I just wanted to know if the facts I had were correct or not and none of the sheep herding teachers wanted to answer me and would throw me out. Now not all my teacher were this way, I had a few great teachers that would answer me and give me new facts to wrestle in my head and create my own opinion, which I believe helps foster the critical thinking of a Wolf and is a necessary step in shedding the Wool.

One of the best examples I can give is my Social Studies teacher, Coach Haight, he would take a Political or Social Subject and write it on the board. He would give us the first part of class to look up info and form our opinion then we would debate it in class and sometimes it took two days to finish the debates. This was a great teaching device because it made the person see both sides of the subject and it made you find the facts instead just taking a book and reciting the knowledge in it. I believe the Wolf Mentality is rooted in being knowledge driven and only accepting facts when they are proven to be real facts and not someone's opinion.

My Family helped me develop this Mentality also because my Mom has always forced the questioning of something that doesn't sound right but at the same time not to question Authority. That right there makes me want to go, but why? I believe the Questioning of Authority is a must in a Wolf, just because someone has a Badge, Title or Holy Book in their hand, this doesn't make them above questioning. If the American Public had questioned Politicians, Bankers and other corrupt people in this Country maybe we wouldn't be in so much debt and Political Corruption. Now when it comes to religion I have a different outlook on things than my Family. My Mom was raised Presbyterian and my Dad was raised Baptist so at a very early age I saw the Bullshit part of Religion. I can't understand why if they believe in the same God that they can't be one Faith. Now I'm not saying that I don't have Faith in a higher power it's just that I have my own view on things as any Wolf should and I don't want to force my Beliefs on Religion on anyone reading this because to become a true Wolf you aren't spoon fed beliefs, you have to form them on your own. As Wolves, we explore different theories and come up with our own take on things and I believe that is the Foundation to the Wolf Mentality.

Now Aggression can be a part of the Wolf Mentality, it certainly is for me but that is because of my upbringing. In my Family its keep, your guard up or you may be taken advantage of. I have always strived to be better than my Parents and my Parents were not bad Parents. It's just that I want to be better not the same. My Dad made damn sure that he wasn't like his Father and for that, I am very grateful. My aggression is from never being able to relax around people in my Family. Some people in my Family have been taking away from me cause of Greed in my Family. These people only wanted my Great Grandmother around for the possessions they might get when she passed away, same thing is going on with my Mom's Mom and if I had the means to change this I would but I don't right now so I try and spend as much time with my Grandparents. Greed is not part of the Wolf Mentality in my opinion. The people who abuse the privilege of having their parent still around will get their final judgment and if I am called to be the death dealer to them so be it. I will do it smiling.

My Grandparents taught me a lot about life, and also helped fuel this Wolf. Cause of my illnesses as a child I was around my Grandparents a lot and I believe this was a blessing. They gave me the knowledge of an older generation that is lost on kids now. Call me old fashioned but I still hold doors open for people, answer Yes, Sir; No, Sir. The only difference now is that I usually do this at Parade Rest. More on why later, I'm sure some already know why.

The Wolf Mentality is also Goal Driven, for example, I was screwed out of going into the Marine Corps by an Officer that forgot what Honor means and now the only way I can be a Marine is to be a Reservist, not my goal. My Goal is to Serve My Country as Active Duty Status so now I am going into the Army because I can be Active Duty, which is my Goal. Goal Driven Mentality; when kicked in the nuts you dust yourself off and try again. Adapt, Improvise and Overcome! Now I know that some will say that I won't be serving my Country but serving the Corporate Masters and Politicians that run this Country but I give this example, even back in the Revolutionary War, Soldiers were not sure if they were fighting on the right side of this newly formed Government of the People and they still put their lives on the line for this out there theory of the time. I believe that I am defending the Constitution, as I am Pledging to do. If I am called to fight in a War I don't agree with completely I will still go and serve and hopefully come back alive. I have this Mentality of Duty; I wanted to be a Fire Fighter before the Military and I would have ran into a burning building to save a Crack head if called to do so.

To simplify my Wolf Mentality comes from my upbringing and always having to fight for what I have. It also comes from Knowledge. Ignorance is only bliss if being a Sheep is what you want to be; to a Wolf Ignorance is Death. Being a Wolf means always looking for the logical answer. Logic is a very important key to the Wolf Mentality; I have met a lot of book smart idiots in my life. A book will not give you the answers, it will give you a one sided view of a subject. If you want to compare Capitalism and Communism, do not just read a book written by a Capitalist taking about Communism read the book on Capitalism and then read a book by Karl Marx about Communism to compare the two sides.

Willingness to improve, Life, Knowledge, etc...

Observe everything

Listen and look carefully for the facts

Forge your own path

Da Nekidgoat

Richard Morgan / Salisbury, N.C

Meet the Pack

Black t-shirts and biker boots
living large just because I could
skull tattoos and a leather coat
my life was never based on luck
got a degree in network technology
wouldn't think that by looking at me
long hair hanging down to my ass
decided to shave it off just like that
Agitation defined this life of mine
standing alone being out of line
Daddy never raised me this way
because I was always the renegade

Da Nekidgoat can be reached at nekidgoat@carolina.rr.com

From Sheep To Wolf

I once believed in the need to satisfy my greed.
The television told me what I really did need.
Politicians passed the laws that I believed right,
and preachers promised me to show me the light.

Until I lost everything and had to live off the land.
I learned then what it took to become a real man.
I grew a thick hide to ward off the cowardly attacks,
learned how to fight hard and to watch my own back.

From the scars of condemnation grew my claws,
I stopped cowering before man made idols and gods.
The fire of my eyes now reflect the heat in my soul,
where once fear had control my heart runs stone cold.

I sheared away the indoctrination of media conformity.
There is no room for thoughts of sheep mentality.
Weakness melts away as spit drips from my fangs,
a howl echoes in the night the strength of my name.
Wolf

Revelation

Baptized in the adversity of insanity
born free but raised to slave in society
to false gods that sells themselves on TV
until realizing you didn't want this to be,
you break free!

No more letting others control your life
stabbed in the back with a corporate knife
nor seeing yourself through another's eyes
no longer backing down but ready to fight
you don't back down.

You are ready to fend off the lies and attacks
the sweat of conformity rolls off your back
black and bruised your integrity is still intact
and yet the flock chooses to ignore the facts
you are their adversary.

You are feeling that you have had enough
and that anything with worth costs blood
that life isn't easy but can be very tough
you find that this path is what you love
you become a wolf.

Life's Journey

I live devoid of any social conformity
an outsider not for fad but individuality
my demeanor is not some sort of mask
I live for the moment not for the past

I look as I do because that is what I choose
I risk it all because I have nothing to lose
my soul isn't marred by media's distortion
but I live free enjoying life's exhilaration

And yet I strive for dreams not fantasy
in my quest I will let no one control me
I do not let prestige make me a slave
I stand alone unchained until it is too late

I look back on my existence and see death
I gave it all I had till there was nothing left
but I don't cower before the grim reaper
because I hear in hell the Jester's laughter

Be Not Satisfied With Being "Normal" But Stand Apart.

Believe not in the convenience of death.
But in the resistance of life's complacency.
Wade not into the calm waters of the river.
Traverse the rapids and explore the depths.

Be alive and feel every pulse of your heart.
Hiding in the shadows will only depress you.
You must leave your footprints in the world.
Be not satisfied with normalcy but stand apart.

Be extraordinary not to others but to yourself.
Truth will only set you free in your own mind.
Do not be a slave to others incompetence.
Trust not in what you see but in what is felt.

Freedom lays in your needs not your desires.
Do not just live, but live to feel each moment.
Wisdom comes not from age but experience.
Start your own revolution and become the fire.

The 1%

Standing on the crevice of responsibility
most of society will take the easy way out
an actions without consequences mentality
but 1% of them will not shut their mouth.

They know the reasons for what they do
and leave no doubt they put up with no shit
they beat themselves until black and blue
but the one thing they won't say is "I quit".

A hardcore heart beats inside this crowd
demanding nothing but to be themselves
they may be a little rough and may be loud
but they accept themselves and fuck the rest.

They believe that what is right is felt within
and must be driven and a little hell bent
so I say with a snarl and a little bit of grin
I am proud to be a part of that one percent.

Superficial Desires

It's not working hard but who's ass you kiss,
it's spending all your money on some TV shit,
it's staying in debt until they lay you in the grave,
if's not what you do but what you twitter to say.

It's depending on poisons the drug companies push,
it's the artificial implants for your boobs and tush, it's
upgrading your phone so you'll have the new app,
or using the newest gadget that vibrates in your lap.

It's the contact lenses that turn your brown eyes blue,
it's hanging out at the mall when there's nothing to do,
it's the fear of pain that made you get a rub on tattoo,
it's that crazy fountain that makes chocolate fondue.

Everybody wants to be a celebrity in their own mind,
because they are scared of the reality they might find,
except for the wolves that don't care for those dreams,
because we know what life cost and what living means.

A Call to Arms

Get off your wolf ass and do something
practice what you preach not less
how are the pups going to learn anything
if you yourself cannot pass the test

to pass the test there must be a fire
and that fire has to burn bright inside
only then will the fire turn into a pyre
there will be no place for fear to hide

and your fire will light the torch hot
your words will the pups truly need
to find in their life what's real or not
to live outside the sheep's mentality

pack nor flock can decide your legacy
that is something you must travel alone
you can not fall into a life of complacency
only then can you call your den a home.

What Is It?

It's not your everyday crap or even hype,
it's a bitchslap in the face of ordinary life,
a revolution born in a defiance kind of type,
a badass attitude that is not afraid to fight.

It's knowing your word is a bond not to be broken,
it can tell what the lies are when they are spoken,
it's doing what needs to be done even if it's a sin,
it's knowing your mistakes and not doing them again.

It's the prowl in the walk that makes them ask why,
the low growl of the voice that puts fear in the eye,
it's living life and it's not letting sleeping dogs lie,
it's the attitude of the pack and a lot of wolf pride.

The Old Wolf

The old wolf lays down his head,
his gray beard touching the ground.
A low laugh escapes his yellowed fangs
at the pups who think they own this town.

You don't have to beat down a sheep,
he snarls out the corner of his mouth,
anybody can beat down a sheep he says,
with eyes glowing red, he then howls out.

Sheep are not worth wasting your bite,
with their worthless fantasies and dreams.
They believe their own arrogant media hype.
They don't even know what living means.

It's not how you die but the reason you lived,
that is the secret of living an honorable life.
To survive the world with integrity intact,
you don't back down when you need to fight.

The Wolf's Prayer

Our brethren, who art in hiding,
Come howling out thy names;
the mutton is done,
thy will be done,
out of the oven and onto the table.
Give us this day the shepherd's head.
And respect us our trespasses,
as we kill the fuckers who trespass against us.
Let forever be the wolven nation,
so when we kick ass we can be primeval.
For ours is the kingdom,
the power, and the glory,
forever and ever, HOWL LOUD!

The Wolf's Path

Nobody said that living a wolf's path was an easy one
you often find yourself alone when sticking to your guns
you give respect when it's due without expecting a return
and you fight till the end because it is not in you to run

some will call you crazy and even more derogatory names
you walk away because you don't have to play their games
it does not matter to you if they hold your actions to blame
excuses are not tolerated because they all sound the same

you're sworn by integrity that bleeds honesty from your pores
when wronged you don't knock but rather break down the door
most are afraid of you but your friends know you are just hardcore
they know that you do not have the time to play society's whore

so to those that walk that path, here are three howls for you
I hoist my goblet and give a toast with my flagon of brew
here is the reverence that you have earned and now are due
you stand apart and live the phrase "to thine own self be true"

The Wolf's Spirit

The greatest strength comes when you hit rock bottom
times when you don't have any one and you don't fit in,
when all hope is lost and you have to pick yourself up,
and you tell yourself that enough is just way too much.

Then you fight back and scratch your way out of the gutter,
rejecting help because you don't want help from another,
standing strong on your own and finding the spirit inside,
to find yourself standing tall and refusing to run away and hide.

So you learn that sometimes you have to practice tough love,
that giving instead of earning is a lot like a pair of handcuffs,
binding one to a life of concession and living in a welfare state,
until you look within to find the strength to change your fate.

You cut loose the chains of suppression that led you there,
you run with the wind not giving a damn what others care,
a life that teaches you, no matter what, you can deal with it,
you feel it, taste it and live it; the strength of the Wolf's Spirit.

Revolution

I raise my voice but nobody pays attention to me,
I'm just one of their slaves in their clueless symphony,
while they live in fantasies without seeing the reality,
indifferent to the intolerance that breeds brutality,
there cannot be freedom under a coward's clinched fist,
there cannot be an age for wolves and sheep to coexist,
when a sheep holds the power it forces the wolf to resist,
till the freedom we remember becomes something we miss,
and so I subsist to torment their exquisite affliction,
the belief that they are invulnerable is just fiction,
a gutless society facing judgment and devastation.
and in purgatory I divine their social destruction,
by fallen ones who refused heaven to hand out hell,
coming out of their dens from whence they had dwelled,
and I perceive others who will answer their call to rebel,
picking up the standard where the champions had fell.

Life

Fate is the journey of crossing the line,
not being normal because it doesn't exit,
boundaries forgotten in the annals of time.
letting the world know that you're pissed.

Reality lives in that determination of anger,
muted only by the strength of the mind,
never satisfied because of righteous hunger,
understood only by brothers of its kind.

Destiny is a black cloud filled with pain,
a malevolence with a wolf's fortitude,
with the intention not to play the game,
for life is not about winning but attitude.

Death is the name of the tattoo on your heart,
and hell is the fantasy of the dreams it brings,
heaven is the willpower to tear enemies apart,
and a true wolf will not bow down to anything!

Mortality

Blood mixed in the droplets of rain
fear is defeated by the growing pain
wounds heal slowly as the years go by
there are no tears as he refuses to die.

Breath is masked in a garbled cough
hands grow numb as old scars grow soft
tattoos fade to a black on gray smear
he can feel it now that death is near.

Mortality is the road to an old man's soul
no one wants him and he has nowhere to go
yet still in defiance he yells to the gods
"You can try to take me but I'll beat the odds."

So he lives every day as if it was his last
if you don't know it by now no need to ask
for every second he lives he feels alive
because Old Wolves don't die, they survive!

Wolves In The Sheep's Nightmare.

Yes, long tooth we are a dying breed,
the kind of men that you no longer see,
living by our word and upon our integrity,
not backing down when we see the need.
We don't live by trends or crave popularity,
and in this world that is indeed a real rarity,
for our blood cries freedom when we bleed,
not bound by rules to force us into conformity.
And here we are together standing strong,
whether we roam in packs or hunt alone,
our lives may be short but our story is long,
few understand us, even fewer hear our song.
So if we die let it be with a clinched fist in the air,
we might have been bastards but we were fair,
we exposed the truth and called out the liars,
we were the wolves in the sheep's nightmare.

Sometimes You Gotta Quit To Be Free

This you say you regret, but I can't just forget,
putting me down because I won't be your clown
things you said to me, brings me up off my knees
don't want an apology, there's a storm inside of me

When you tried to muzzle me, I tried to tell you to let it be
you threatened my livelihood, said you'd fire me if you could
I couldn't stand it no more, so I walked out the front door
now you think the problem is gone but it has only begun

I'll fight back just for my respect, I'll fight to the death
tired of you greedy whore, now I am closing the door
you have no control over me, this I'll make you believe
there's only one thing I need and you're too blind to see

Justification without retribution is not my redemption
nor is it my only salvation found in strong subordination
I have sacrificed what I needed in my quest to be free
so I'll be who I want to be and take sole responsibility

If I am damned for what I do then it's for me and not you
I stand by my word, that is why I don't fit in your world
so don't think that you can ever be a wild free wolf like me
I have beaten off your attack and I ain't going back

DA NEKIDGOAT (RICHARD MORGAN)

Castration By Indoctrination

It starts early as we send our kids to school,
where conformity is taught and lessons are cruel,
teach to the test becomes the mantra of death,
critical thinking is lost and only zombies are left.

Socrates and Plato are replaced by Dick and Jane,
Fo Shizzle becomes grammar like the rain in Spain,
while gunshots signify the end of a heated debate,
no wonder teachers and parents are scared to death.

Where 25 to life is the only math students can understand,
where dumbass studs believe Vegas whores are the best in this land
and the only reality is the use of video games to ease the social pain,
Education has become Indoctrination in this twisted game.

Wolf Wannabe

You say you're still running against the wind,
trying to stand apart and trying not to blend in.
with your black t-shirt and long ass black hair,
walking in footsteps that's already been there.

You'd rather be an open sinner than a false saint.
Well saints commit sin at the sound of my name.
You say you don't give idle threats but predictions.
I control your future because of your idle condition.

You say you're the toughest mutha' in the valley.
The mutha' who made that valley was fuckin 'me.
Think you're the one your mom warned you about?
Well I am the mutha' who turned your mother out.

You ask who is this arrogant one, this painted face clown.
I'm the one who steps up when everyone else steps down.
The secret of my name is said in respect under this roof.
I am the evolution of the Jester into the wicked Wolf.

Dancing To Our Own Song

I walk down the street, you cross to the other side,
you wish I would crawl into a dark hole and hide,
but to your disgust I am not going to go anywhere,
this isn't your world and I don't really give a care.

Pump those fist and howl all night long, "Fuck you!"
wolves run together and we stick together like glue,
you mess with us and you'll see how cruel we can be,
when you try to stick us in your cookie cutter society.

You want to save the world, then we can show you how,
you just have to listen to the words in our low growl,
you can't be free when you live in a life of constant greed,
and keep it up; we'll give you the ass kicking you need!

So it'll be you running down the street into that dark hole,
and it's your own fault if you want to give away your soul,
to the media whores and the next big thing to come along,
as for us wolves we will sing and dance to our own song!

The Anthem

It's a Wolf Revolution and it's coming,
hitting the streets with fists pumping,
voices shouting and feet stomping,
our time is now and it's all or nothing.

We know no fear but righteous anger,
only retribution can satisfy our hunger,
and we refuse to fit in a sheep's world,
because we stand tall and live by our word.

United as one, we will hold our ground,
bust open the doors, unleash the hounds,
and what once was lost can now be found,
our knees don't bend, we won't bow down.

In our hands we hold strength and integrity,
in our minds we know personal responsibility,
in our souls we realize truth and accountability,
in our hearts we know we can change this society.

Religion

The quest for redemption lies not in the heart of men,
but in the minds of those who defy salvation's grace.
For salvation freely given is not worth the price of the sin.
Heaven must be earned else it becomes just a waste.

The judgment in a god's condemnation is of no worth,
when how one lives is more important than why one lives,
when one's obedience to one's belief becomes a curse.
What is more important, how much one takes or one gives?

Is the soul of a man defined by actions left on his legacy?
How can his legacy live on to those that find him unknown?
Or is his legacy etched on his tombstone in the cemetery?
Judged by the seeds he had sown, or what he has become?

So live life to the fullest based on the belief of mortality,
because forever dies in the eyes of a quiescent man,
become more than a sheep in a flock of this society,
do not become just another footprint in the sand.

Growing Old

Chances are one foots on the edge, the others in the grave,
I crossed a lot of lines and I got a bunch of dues to be paid,
and maybe I should start caring about the bad things I said,
but that ain't me because I have no regrets for the life I led.

The fire I feel inside burns like the hell I find that's outside,
what's the use of running when there's nowhere to hide,
so I'll stay right here in this place till that hell freezes over,
growing stronger knowing that life isn't meant to last forever.

Am I scared of death you ask? I have to say hell yeah truthfully,
and that's make me want to enjoy this life more completely,
heaven nor hell makes much sense on where I want to go,
I'll just reap the flowers and the weeds of the seeds I'd sown.

Day by day really means minute by minute to an old wolf,
and it seems that he keeps on taking and nothings enough,
it's not money and success that seems to brighten his day,
but it's his family and friends that lightens his fur of gray.

Wannabe Warning

The subjugation to addiction cannot be easily broken,
when one falls back into the beliefs that were spoken,
you search for what was taught since you were a child,
where obedience was not questioned nor asked why.

How do you think for yourself when others decide for you?
Can you break out of the mentality to comply with what to do?
Is the sound of a different drummer muffled by your fear?
Are you afraid to realize your sovereignty when it is so near?

Others think it is as easy as a knife cuts through soft butter.
that a sheep can get rid of its wool and become another.
But the seeds of a wolf are bred into the values of the soul,
not any sheep can break out of the flock and into the fold.

You can paint your body and say you have changed your ways,
but a wolf can tell what is real and what is only sheep made,
so don't try to fool the pack by displaying balls you don't have,
if you do, we will just have to send you back into sheep rehab

I'm Just A Sic' Fuck

I'm just a sic fuck
in a sic fuckn' world
and to tell the truth
you're a sic fuck too

got the sic fuck blues
paid our sic fuckn' dues
played by all the rules
got played like a fool

and still they play fuckn' games
in their own sic fuckn' names
takes the credit not the blame
nothing changes, stays the same

time to take this sic fuckn' land
out of their sic fuckin' hands
into the world of black and blue
and tell them "Fuck You"

'Twas The Night Before A Wolf's Christmas

Twas the night before Christmas, and all through the forum,
not a creature was stirring, not even Thorin.
The release forms hung on the whiteboard with care,
in hopes that the mailman soon would be there.

The wolves were nestled all snug in their dens,
wondering when the slaughtering would begin.
And Ronin in his chair with a shotgun on his lap,
had just settled his brains for a long winter's nap.

When out on the lawn there arose such a clatter,
but it was nothing but Theo emptying his bladder.
Still Randal flew away to the window like a flash,
tore open the shutters and threw up the sash.

The moon on the breast of the new-fallen snow
gave the lustre of mid-day to objects below.
When, what to old wondering eyes should appear,
an old truck with eight little sheep shivering in fear.

With a tough old driver with a worn out mop,
we knew in a moment it must be Swatcop.
Slower than turtles the wolves they came,
and he whistled, and shouted, and called them by name!

"Now Viking! now, Reina! now, Goat and Metalhead!
Get your asses up now, out of your beds!
To the top of the porch! to the top of the wall!
Now slash away! Slash away! Kill them all!"

And then, in a twinkling, A Jester jumped on the roof
with a prancing and pawing he stomped his hoof.
As we drew in our heads, and was turning around,
down the chimney He came with a big bound.

He was dressed all in black, from his head to his foot,
and his clothes were all tarnished with ashes and soot.
A bundle of lambchops he had flung on his back,
and he looked like a peddler, just opening his pack.

His eyes-how they twinkled! his dimples how wicked!
His cheeks and nose looked like he was pickled!
His droll mouth was drawn up showing his fangs,
you could tell he wasn't feeling any kind of pain.

He spoke not a word, but went straight to his work,
and filled all the plates, then turned with a jerk.
And laying his finger aside he picked his nose,
and giving a nod, up the chimney he rose!

He sprang to the truck; to the wolves he gave a whistle,
and away he flew like the down of a thistle.
But we heard him exclaim, 'ere he drove out of sight,
"You ain't shit if you back down, so put up a good fight!"

Shotgun Shells (Jingle Bells)

Dashing through the snow
Looking for some sheep to slay
This one thing I know
I'm going to bag me one today
That old buckshot will sting
lighting up his ass
What fun it is to laugh and sing
While slaying sheep tonight

Oh, shotgun shells, shotgun shells
Blasting all the way
Oh, what fun it is to hunt
With a bunch of sheep to slay
Oh, shotgun shells, shotgun shells
Blasting all the way
Oh, what fun it is to hunt
Sheep on Christmas Day

To The Writers Of This Book

The man in the mirror is just a shadow,
and the words in his pen may seem radical,
writing of standing on his own in mystery,
challenging fate and denying his own history.

Where he once was silent, now he is loud,
not afraid to fight or stand out in a crowd,
some mistake the Jester in him for a clown,
and growing up he has always been put down.

He was pushed to the edge and picked up the pen,
and he found his voice to begin life all over again,
writing of the strength that an outcast acquires,
separating the truth from the media whores and liars.

Yeah that's you in the mirror, the shadow in gray,
writing of old times and sometimes a new day,
telling stories of a fallen brother or a lost cause,
I never knew so much could come from a wolf's paw!

Enlightened One

Meet the Pack

I am Enlightened One. I have known about Stalking the Flock for a few years now and decided in May of 2010 to actually join in the forums and meet the wolves that I'm now glad to call my friends. If this is your first glance into the world of nonconformity, and you have decided you like what you see, then I would suggest registering in the forums and speaking with us and also taking a look at Thorin's works as well. If not, then go back to your life of blissful ignorance...

If you want to know more about me, contact me on stalkingtheflock. com or my personal website www.enlightenedwolf.wordpress. com. It isn't updated often though.

Bullets

✦ In times of great strife, only those with a clear mind and a strong will, will stand triumphant.

✦ Live your life trying to better the lives of the others around you... Not just the one that signs the paychecks.

✦ Don't just bite the hand that feeds... Tear that motherfucker off and give the man a grin so bloody and menacing, that he will think twice before trying to strike you down again...

✦ If actions were guns, and words their ammunition lots of people in this world would be left with nothing but ammunition because most people speak about their "actions" and they never come to fruition.

✦ Theories lead to thinking, actions lead to success.

Life

We all know that death is our inevitable fate...This fact rules most people's lives and constrains them to a life lived within the bounds of normal society, instead of living their life to the fullest. You can't live your life in fear of what could happen or else you doom yourself to a life void of love, happiness, thrill and most importantly self-fulfillment. Many will think that when I say live your life to the fullest, that I mean to go out and strap on a parachute and jump out of a plane or go climb Mt. Everest. On the surface, this is true. Hiding yourself from the world in fear of death or pain isn't a way to live. This isn't the whole of the concept of truly living. You have to think past the adrenaline and look into your soul to find what you need to make your life whole. The love of a significant other, thinking for yourself rather than letting others does it for you or even fulfilling a childhood dream. This is what living your life to the fullest means. Not hiding your primal desires to avoid being ridiculed or shunned for your individuality. If you truly want to live for yourself and not for others, you will ignore these taunts and use them to build yourself up. The sheep will use what power their closed minds have to ridicule you because their small minds can't see anything outside what society tells them is normal.

Ftrdsrk

Meet the Pack

George B. AKA ftrdsrk, sworn leader of the Fetard pack, is a man of few words. He is inclined to let his actions speak for him. An observer he learns most by watching. He would like to thank Thorin and the others for helping him shed the last of his wool and to let him roam freely through the Badlands.

We Hunger

We hunger for pride, they accept humility

We hunger for knowledge, they accept ignorance

We hunger for strength, they accept sufferance

We hunger for life, they accept existence

We hunger for success, they accept failure

We hunger to provide, they accept welfare

We hunger for freedom, they accept control

We hunger for advancement, they accept barriers

We hunger for courage, they accept weakness

We hunger for territory, they accept boundaries

We hunger to lead, they accept following

We hunger for rebellion, they accept complacence

We hunger for the pack, they accept the flock

Bullets

✦ If you do not have anything to offer society do not be surprised when society offers you nothing back.

✦ Here is the church here is the steeple open it up and find the sheeple.

✦ More is accomplished when we live up to our own expectations rather than those of others.

✦ Have you ever looked at someone and just know that cartoon bubble above their head has nothing in it.

✦ If you chose to judge me and get no response, it is safe to assume I do not respect your opinion.

✦ If everywhere you go, and everything you do, things seem to go wrong, please consider the common denominator.

Jordan "Greywolf" Jackson

A Single Howl

Running through trees as sparse as we
Our kind, the numbered few.
With foggy breath and gleaming coat
With glinting claw and tooth.
With head thrown back and moon up high
A lone and fearsome sound
May all the sheep now fear the wolves
Who gather to the howl.

The Toast

Our kind's been discontinued now
And none of us emerged unscathed
But scars, I hear, can make men tough
And unhurt men are seldom brave
So raise your voice and give a cry
There's still time yet to conquer fear
And through what comes we will survive
So long as we have brothers near.

The Wolf's Cry

Trembling flock of hoof and wool
Are huddled by the sound.
The stalking pack of tooth and claw
Run swift along the ground.
Moonlight shines all through the trees
A darting flash of grey.
The flock trembles 'neath their tree
Who will die today?
The wolves look on in dire contempt
At the shuffling of the lambs
These animals so quick to trust
The shepherd's lying hands.
These things who treat their keepers
As messiah, master, god.
Who spend their useless lives away
Just doing as they're told.
The alphas slow and keep well back.
Glaring at the sight.
The shepherd comes to tend his flock
And sleep with them tonight.
The alpha's know, there'll come a day
When wolves will rule again.
And run the land the way they did
Before invading men.
With head thrown back and jaw agape
They give the world a fright.
The wolf's cry does ensure one thing:
No shepherds sleep tonight.

Hunt

Sing a song from long ago
whose meaning disappears
A hearty howl of anger
that has fallen on deaf ears

Tell a story of the past
that all have now forgot
a saga of the warrior
whose body's left to rot

Let me hear of honor
and the pride of a man's word
Let me see the dedication
that is written with a sword

When did people fall apart
And bleat aloud their woe?
When did it become okay
to sacrifice our code?

When did men forget their honor
Just money in the bank?
When did we learn that what we have
is what determines rank?

There was a thing once long ago
That claimed the false of tongue
That trampled o'er the oathbreaker
and scared all of our young.

I call an end for all of them
And I raise my howl high
I wait to hear an answer
So the Wild Hunt may ride.

Lycaon

Not Like You

From within the safety
Of your flock
You stare at me
You point, and mock

You laugh at my clothes
You laugh at my hair
You criticize the way
I simply don't care

About how you think
I should live my life
With my own rules for living,
My middle fingers held high

I only smile
At your eyes full of scorn
Too strong to submit
To your societal norms

I see the big picture
How you're a slave to the game
"You laugh cause I'm different
I laugh cause your the same"

Box Of Fear

I sit down in front of my TV
It says to be paranoid of everyone I see
Especially those who don't look like me
For our enemies are not only across the sea
"For your safety, some liberty must be halted
To prevent our Homeland from being assaulted
Security, over freedom, must be exalted
We will defend freedom and stand undaunted."

A suited man issues warnings grave
"If you don't submit your rights, you'll become a slave
To a faceless enemy, hiding in a cave
You will remain safe, if you don't question us and do as we say."

Changing the channel, I still see lies
Fear mongering tactics flashed before my eyes
"If we don't take precautions, we will meet our demise
So into your private lives we must pry."

"Privacy is a privilege you cannot afford
When evil can strike on its on accord
You're either with us or not, so you better be on board
We must all sacrifice something, to combat the evil horde"

I pick up my remote, trembling with anger
"Can this Orwellian double speak get any stranger?"
I don't buy into their manufactured danger
And I refuse to submit or make my words any tamer

At their manipulations and lies, I can only scoff
So, I stand up from my couch, and turn the box of fear off

Maxwell D. Birkholz Jr.

Bullets

✦ If Darwin were alive today he would be disappointed that the theory of evolution doesn't apply to sheeple

✦ For every ounce of truth that's out there, there is a ton of bullshit piled on top of it. Knowledge is the shovel that will help you dig past the bullshit in order to reach the truth.

✦ Those that choose to be consumers will undoubtedly be consumed themselves.

✦ When you wear the mask of deceit you're doomed to be cut by the ice cold blade of karma.

✦ If being normal means being like everybody else, consider me a freak.

✦ If you follow blindly you will never see the path to your true self.

✦ To find your true self you must make your own path; to follow another will only burden your journey.

Mr. McCoy

Grey Hairs

When the leader of the pack turns old and grey,
his days are numbered. It's to be that way.

But his growl is still loud and strong; His respect still stands
regardless of natures plans.
As he rest his eyes and his joints are in pain, that's when the
sheep try to play there games.

They think he's too old to put up a fight, But that is when they
should be aware of his bite.
for he will lash out your throat without even a twitch, and will
leave you to bleed out face down in a ditch, As he walks away
with your blood on his face, let it be known he put the sheep in
there place.

R.J Olsen

Prayer

I pray,

For the day their world comes crashing down,

When their bodies fall into the ocean and drown,

I pray,

For the day the ground opens up and they fall,

When their bodies collapse so far down they can't crawl,

I pray,

For the day meteors crash and no one survives,

When their ignorance costs them their lives,

I pray,

For the ignorant and stupid,

For the hypocrites and the sheeple,

For the hopeless apathetic and the rest of these pitiful fucking people.

I pray.

Refuser Of The Label

I am not a goth,

I am not a prep,

I am not an emo,

I am not a burnout,

I am a refuser of the label.

I am not nerd,

I am not a redneck,

I am not a jock,

I am not a gangster,

I am not a punk,

I am a refuser of the label.

I am free,

I am me,

Who I choose to be!

Bullets

✦ Truth and bliss rarely coincide

✦ Often times I will let my fist speak for me- put a pen in it and I will let it scream for me.

✦ Insanity is only an opinion

✦ I don't know what I find more repulsive, a rebel without a cause, or a cause without a rebel.

✦ I am not your sinner nor your saint, I am my own. I am not your angel nor you demon, I am my god.

✦ The sheeple are not creations of nature, but rather products of themselves

✦ My fist shall be my hammer, smashing through any wall of adversity I encounter. My mind shall be the force driving it.

✦ Herd mentality is like fish hooks in the flesh, either rip them out painfully, or become blinded and bound forever.

✦ When death comes knocking on my door, I will fight him with every ounce of strength I have in me, I shall grasp onto life like a lion onto his prey, but when I know my time is finally up, I will let death in without resistance and without fear

✦ It is easy to become blinded by the light; however, one must remember that you cannot see in the dark either.

✦ Before one soars to the sun, he must first strengthen his wings.

◆ The one that has peacefully live in his chains has surely earned his metal.

◆ You are only a slave to the master of adversity until you snarl back at him and take his position.

Are you hungry?

Picture your mind as a dinner plate. Picture any food going on your plate as the opinions and beliefs you gain. The only things on your plate from birth are the etchings engraved by nature. As you grow food is constantly thrown onto your plate. Perhaps, the bread on your plate is from your mother and father. Perhaps the vegetable lying there are from other family. Perhaps the fruit is from the television. No matter where it is from, it is there nonetheless. Your mind is not free, for it is weighed down by the food of others. To free your mind, you must empty your plate. Perhaps you will notice the etchings from birth have since faded. Take no more food from others! But rather hunt your own! Seek your own truths. Perhaps you may even scavenge some of the earlier thrown away food. Your plate will not fill itself. You must seek and hunt. Avoid any poisons. By emptying your plate, you will find yourself hungry, hungry for knowledge! And gathering and hunting your own food is the only way to keep your mind free and curiosity satisfied. So I ask you, are you hungry?

R.W. Smith

Meet The Pack

R.W. Smith is a 27 year old college student working towards his Bachelors in Applied Technology based out of Spokane, WA. His personal website is http://www.randomparadox.com

Awakening

Throughout this book, you have heard other wolves tell you the hows and the why's regarding the adoption of the wolf philosophy. The ways to be proactive to become a free, individual thinker. Unfortunately, not everybody, especially the heavily sheep-minded, can take those steps themselves. Truth be told, my initial foray into the wolf philosophy wasn't through any actions of my own. Many of the events that turned me into the thinker I am today were beyond my control. In essence, I was 'awakened' by others.

Many times in life, ideas, facts, and opinions get thrown in your direction. Whether you hear them from your parents, the media (mainstream or otherwise, whatever that means), friends, or concerned parties, some of them should make you stop and think about your own ideas. For the heavily sheep-minded, these new ideas can take time to break through their thick shielding. Many will shrug off the new ideas as being wrong and head off on their merry way. Even if these ideas being thrown at them made a dent, the dent eventually fixes itself and the shield is just as good as it ever was. To make that dent permanent takes a lot of ammunition, time, and effort.

This is why many wolves will tell you that you need to be proactive in order to break down that shielding. They believe that one cannot rely on others. But this is not always the case. Instead of being proactive, or receiving a barrage of ideas that one's shield cannot stand up to, sometimes it only takes a few armor-piercing bullets. An armor-piercing bullet is an idea so powerful that it shoots through the shield and makes the sheep question his previously held idea, without much effort from the shooter. Once the bullet has made it through, the sheep will start to question other things as well. Not through any means of his own, but due to some chain reaction set off by the bullet. It is this chain reaction that I call the awakening.

For me, the first bullet that pierced my armor was made of metal. Heavy metal. For most of my young life I avoided heavy music. Somewhere in my brain a seed was planted by my parents, and probably various television programming, that metal was bad as were the people that listened to it. Well, one day I had a friend basically sit me down and force me to listen to two bands. A pair of famous '80's metal bands. Initially, I said no. I told my friend that I didn't want to listen to crap music. That shield was up. I forgot exactly how he got me to listen, but I did. And the bullet was fired.

The music resounded with me. I fell in love with one band's 'man vs. machine' themes, and one of them became one of my favorite songs. The other band had an album that I listened to a lot. More importantly, I questioned what else I had been told was a lie, not proactively, but as a reaction. The world wasn't black and white anymore. Things were to be questioned if they were to be fully understood.

This idea, this armor-piercing bullet, won't be the same with everyone. The idea that pierces ones armor may bounce off another's without so much as a scratch. Most often, this idea will hit them on a personal level. Personal things aren't so easy to shrug off. Often, it will take more than one of these bullets. It took several of them for me. Most of them I received while serving in the Army. Without going into too much detail, those bullets came in the form of experiencing many different cultures and ideas, as well as listening to and carrying out terrible leadership ideas and orders that made no logical sense.

When those bullets made enough holes in my shield, the shield became useless and the sheep in me threw it away. I was finally open to new ideas, opinions, and I allowed the hard facts to change my perspective. It wasn't long before I had adopted the wolf philosophy. I critically think about everything now. Every story has multiple sides, and I take interest in the roots of one's ideas. I'm not afraid to look into new ideas either.

The awakening process may be a fast one, or it can be slow. It may be conscious or subconscious. When the person receives that first bullet, they initially question the idea related to that bullet. The idea mulls around in their head and they think about it. They start to think about it from multiple angles, and they tackle every question they have about it. Eventually, the idea is fully understood. This full understanding may come a few moments after the bullet, or it may come years after.

After that understanding comes, the next part of the process is the person beginning to question the source or sources of his original idea. If it was their parents, the question becomes 'what else were they wrong about?' If it was a societal one, the person asks 'why does society believe these things.' The person starts to take a closer look at things, if only because of a new found curiosity.

The final part of the process is looking into things that this person does not fully understand. Things he would normally shy away from out of fear. Sometime during this part of the process is when the awakened starts to act on his own. This is the most vital stage in adopting the wolf philosophy. At this point, the person is now fully capable of taking all the actions he needs to take. This is why it sometimes takes more than one armor-piercing bullet. Either the shield will come off, or the person continues to wear it, choosing to be a follower and live in happy ignorance.

It is my firm belief that no wolf will ever be able to awaken a collective group of sheep. If sheep are to be awakened, they have to be awakened on an individual level. For a true wolf, that should be the easy part. A wolf can easily analyze an individual person's ideas and belief system. Given enough time with that person, a wolf can find the right bullet for the job and fire. Now I won't be so bold to say that it is the duty of every wolf to awaken the sheep. Giving a wolf a duty is undermining the whole 'think for yourself' aspect of being a wolf. Some wolves are happy with awakening others, and have made it their duty. Some wolves are content with letting the sheep be sheep. Both are entirely acceptable.

The awakening is a gift. Initially, being awoken may feel like a curse. You suddenly have no interest in keeping up with trends of the day. You no longer participate in activities simply because your friends are doing it. You no longer subscribe to ideas from politicians, teachers, parents, and other authority figures because they are the authority. You lose friends and lose 'respect' from others. Over time, you will realize it was worth it. Wolves tend to be more successful. By this I mean they feel more successful, as success should not be gauged by any standard other than your own. They are able to live life their way, and aren't tied to doing things the way society wants them to. You get to live life for you. What's not to like about that?

Randal

Meet the Pack

R andal, also known as "Long tooth" on the forum, is the oldest member of the forum, as far as anyone will admit. He can't remember being anything but a wolf all his life thanks, in part, to his parents who raised him to be independent and think for himself.

Randal has been married for 35 years and has 6 kids, 4 grandkids. His wife, who is the polar opposite of him, still questions her choice but seems to love him anyway (but there are days….). Randal would be lost without his family and talks to them daily. Regardless of where he is in the world, he always knows where home is.

His background is as wild and varied as his thinking. He worked pre-hospital emergency medicine (paramedic) for the better part of 20 years before working in the oil and gas industry. Since the mid-90s, Randal has worked in safety around the world and to date has worked in 14 countries. Currently he is working in Egypt at a petrochemical plant.

As either a result of Randal's amazing ability to adapt or learn or, more likely, his rampant ADD, he has worked in the following professions: paramedic, deputy sheriff, animal control supervisor, delivered pizzas, sold postcards, delivered telephones, worked offshore as a medic/safety puke, cleaned up a slaughter house, drove an armored car, private security officer and done screen printing. He has also owned 4 businesses with various degrees of success, or lack of same.

A preacher at a church Randal used to go to told Randal's wife that "Randal was the most unconventional thinker he had ever known". To put it another way, Randal says that he has been thinking outside of the box for so long, he forgot where the damn thing is.

In his spare time Randal is a fledgling writer of essays and poetry, listens to music (he is still a metal head) and reads an eclectic variety of books.

Randal can be reached at: texian@inbox.com or texas.grok@gmail.com. His website and personal blog is: www.hardcoremind.com.

Inspiration

Why do you say I'm an inspiration?
Why do you hold me in admiration?
Why do you need someone to look up to?
The potential to be a wolf resides within you.

Don't try to be like me, be what resides within
Think for yourself; look deep under your skin
Do you want to be like me? Then fuck off!
Imitating another is the ultimate selloff.

I'm nobodies' role model, don't look up to me
Inspiration comes from what you want to be
If a wolf is your goal, look to no one but yourself
It is not something learned from a book on a shelf

If you have to look up to another for inspiration
Then your journey to being a wolf will end in frustration
Inspiration comes not from another but from the wolf within
You have the potential to break from the flock, to win

This will come through a struggle with the greatest foe
Someone who will fight to maintain the status quo
This someone is yourself, your greatest enemy
To the sheep within, breaking from the flock is blasphemy

The inner struggle is ultimately between the wolf and the sheep
inside
Unleash the wolf to fight, from the battle it will proudly stride
The wolf will always win in a fight with the sheep inside
You only have to release your wolf that within is tied

End Of Days

The old wolf looked back, his pack had faded away
Where had the time gone, was this the end of days?
He remembered when his pups were by his side
He remembered a time when his pack was his pride

Time had moved on and the old wolf was left behind
His pack had moved on, his life now aside
Had he done the right things? Had he raised them strong?
Had he raised his pups right or had he been wrong?

Only time would tell and perhaps he would be dead
Before his pups chose the right way and remembered what he had said
Our legacy is what we leave behind with those that we love
It is seen in their resilience when push comes to shove

Legacy is not about the material things we leave behind
It is about love, honor, duty, and having the strength to be kind
It is about being remembered as someone that took no guff
It is about being remembered as being loving but also tough

The old wolf shook his mane and cleared the cobwebs from his head
He realized that his days were numbered and soon he would be dead
But he realized deep inside that he had done right and good
He could now die with honor knowing in his pack's eyes where he stood

The Man In Black

A man in black, a wicked jester on his shirt
Walks down the street his senses alert
He sees the sheep and smells their fear
He feeds on this and at them can only sneer

"Why he must be evil! I must stay away from him!"
The sheep move to one side, almost all of them
But there is one sheep that looks the wolf in the eye
The wolf sees one sheep that today might not die

"This sheep has promise" says the wolf to himself
This sheep did not shy away but in and of itself,
This did not make the sheep worthy of living past today
This did not hold the wolves' wrath at bay

There was something else about this member of the flock
Something in its eyes that seemed to mock
Something in its eyes that the wolf saw as kindred
A glint to this sheep's eyes that was a bit blood red

I'll talk to this sheep said the wolf to himself
I'll see if his words match this pride of oneself
The sheep waited as the wolf came close and wary
The sheep thought that this wolf was not so scary

The sheep saw the promise, the hope in his eye
The sheep saw that the flock was wrong and turned in good bye
The sheep's wool began to change from fluffy to course
The sheep teeth grew long and his words full of force

That day one from the flock became one of the pack
Soon it would be his day to stalk the flock and then attack

But he would look out for that one sheep with no fear
He too would talk to this sheep and not sneer
This tale is for my pack of brothers and sisters
When you see a flock, look for the resistors
Look for the sheep that show some potential
Their white wool, in this case, inconsequential

Our strength is in numbers and our numbers should increase
Our enemy is vast and our only chance is to defeat, not make peace
We grow our numbers through our examples and words
We grow our pack by changing sheep, and they leaving the herds

So when you are prowling a mall or a store
Look at the sheep; see if with one you have a rapport
Use your words and your actions to sway them
Change them from sheep to wolves, these few, don't slay them

Hysteria Darkly Flowers

The sheep hear the words and they are afraid
We have enemies, we must continue the crusade
Our enemies hate us; they hate us for our freedoms
They will attack us while hiding safe in their kingdoms

They sheep are steered this way and that
The sheep are controlled with scary videos to look at
The herders control the flock electronically
Their words coming from the speakers sardonically

The herder's dogs and staff have been replaced
By an electronic media that the sheep have embraced
The sheep no less controlled than before
The sheep selling out their freedoms and beg for war

The sheep are enslaved despite no physical shackles
The pack growls and howls, it only increasing their hackles
The pack circles the flock, staying in the shadows
The pack barks and nips but the flock still follows

The flock follows the herders to the edge of the abyss
Always trusting the herders, never realizing what is amiss
The wolves fall back, having tried to change the destiny
They tried to change the sheep, hoped they would mutiny

But the flock always follows until finally at the edge
They get a glimpse something is wrong and try to hedge
But it is too late; the back of the flock continues to follow
The abyss is below, all too ready to swallow

The flock falls to their death, bleating as they plummet
The pack stands growling at the edge of the summit

The pack tried to warn them, wolves to the sheep
But the words of the pack the sheep would not heed or keep
The flock is now dead but more sheep take their places
The herders still control the flock, same type, different faces
The pack still prowls and growls at the sheep, at the flock
The pack still uses its words to educate or perhaps mock

The pack knows that in the end the herders will win
This flock will be controlled, sheep die, their numbers thin
But the pack will always fight when there is evil that threatens
And the pack will teach through its howls to whoever will listen

Last One Standing

The field was barren, the sky was grey
A sheep was alone, from the flock a stray
The lone wolf entered the field from the forest
On his body, scars from past battles and conquest

The sheep had lost its way, a stray from the flock
But it thought itself strong, of different stock
The sheep saw the wolf but thought itself a worthy foe
A war of words and ideals, things it would know

The sheep threw the first blow, hoping it was fatal
Something he had heard on TV, something on cable
Another's opinion, the sheep took as his own
With this feeble weapon, the first blow was thrown

The wolf parried easily, this attempt at a fight
To defend against this attempt feeble, his effort slight
The wolf fought back with his mind, thoughts of his own
The sheep was staggered, sunk to the ground with a groan

The sheep tried to attack again with something from the news
The attack was easily batted way by the wolf, now amused
The wolf thought this funny, this attempt at combat by a sheep
The sheep thought it sport but the wolf fights for keeps

The wolf struck again, using logic and clear thinking
The sheep cried out in pain, further to the ground sinking
The sheep called for mercy, he was no match for this creature
He saw the wolf as an enemy but the wolf was a teacher

Pain was the lesson today, the pain of opening his mind
He would survive this battle but never be content with his own kind

The wolf would leave him alive, injured, in agony
What would come next would be something of an irony

He would later think back on that day, the battle
The day his beliefs were challenged and violently dismantled
The day his coat began to change, from wool to fur
The day the counterattack was so quick, really a blur

The day he realized that the life of a sheep was the wrong path
Something that would never have happened if not for the wolf's wrath
A day never forgotten, he never returned to the flock
Now their antics were silly, he could only now mock
The day the sheep became a wolf, days that are too few
A day that changed his life, everything now anew
The day the wolf was the last one standing
The day the sheep became a wolf, a new life gladly accepting

The Fear Within

Everyone has fears within
Wolves or sheep, this has always been
But to the sheep, it becomes a shield
Something to hide behind and yield

The sheep needs their fear, their dark enemies
It gives them excuses, reasons for their anxieties
They can cower and hide behind the government
But to the wolf, this attitude is abhorrent

To the wolf fear is something to confront
Something to kill after a long hunt
Fear to the wolf is an opportunity to prove something
Defeating fear a goal worth achieving

Fear is the challenge to gets the wolf running
But unlike the sheep, towards the fear using his cunning
Cunning to defeat and destroy his fear
Courage to crush, to rip, to jeer

Fear comes to us all, just like death
But to the wolf, he greets it, fighting to his last breath

I Don't Care

I don't care
I don't care what is on TV
It means little to me
Your latest gadget that thrills you
Just makes me want to kill you

Who is voted off the tribe
Which politician has accepted a bribe
Who won an award as actress
Your priorities are aimless

You care about only yourself
Your morals have been put on a shelf
You care more about your gadgets
Than people being killed by bayonets

You have cancelled compassion
You are more concerned with fashion
Your fancy clothes are made by near slaves
Who work themselves into a pauper's grave

You stuff your faces with fast-food
A price to your health being accrued
Children starving slowly in Africa
People killing themselves quickly in America

I don't care what you think is right
I don't care what you watch at night
I don't care who is your hero
Your whole life to me is a zero

I care about my friends and family
I care about how my kids grow up to be
I care about helping people truly in need
I care about keeping my personal creed

My creed is simple, my words you should heed
I will take care of my own and not cave to greed
I will fight to the death for what is right
I will not quietly go into that long dark night

You sheep with your superficial needs
Your morals and values you readily concede
I do not care what happens to the flock
As you die, my pack and I will standby and mock

We Are All Born Wolves

The day we are born, we are the same in one way
The soul inside of a wolf, a predator not prey
If our parents are wolves and raise us as one
We will grow to be strong and freely run

If we are brought up strong in body and mind
Taught to think for ourselves, not to be blind
If mistakes we are allowed to make so we might learn
We will discover that life is tough, lessons are stern

When we become adults, full grown wolves we will be
Our lessons learned, perhaps scars for all to see
We will be strong, running with packs or alone
We will be individuals, not like sheep who are clones

But if our parents are part of the flock of sheep
We will grow as one of the flock, our minds asleep
We will be weak in body and soul as well
Something about us that we won't usually quell

Our parents will protect us from what they think are dangers
Games like dodge ball, to be scared of every stranger
Any mark on our bodies might get infected or create a scar
To the doctor we are taken, lest the trauma goes too far

Our wolf soul is gradually lessened as we grow older
Our stride turns feeble and weak instead of bolder
Our parents think they are doing what is best to protect
To raise you different than they were raised they reject

One day the full grown sheep goes out on their own
Another member of the flock, just another drone

Perhaps one day a bit of the wolf spirit might kindle
But because of the flock it will surely dwindle

The sheep may look up from the flock to see a vision
To see a wolf strong and proud, the sheep may face indecision
Could he still be like that? Possibly to go from wool to fur?
Perhaps a bit of the wolf's spirit deep inside will stir.

If the sheep is willing the wolves are happy to help
To a proud adult, the wolves have raised many a whelp
But the sheep has to be willing to go against all he was taught
Against his upbringing, there is a battle to be fought
The day may come when that sheep wins his war
When his heart will be strong, his spirit will soar
When his wool is shed for a coat of glorious fur
Memories of being a sheep and the flock just a blur

When that day comes, all the wolves with him will rejoice
The howls of victory over the sheep rising in one voice
The new wolf will be welcomed into the pack
The next flock will be stalked and attacked

Perhaps more sheep will be turned to wolves in coming days
Perhaps the continuous loss of our freedoms held at bay
But as long as the wolf spirit is turned into a sheep
Children to adults will no longer growl but only bleat

Raise your children to be strong and let them make mistakes
Foster the spirit of the wolf in your pup when that spirit awakes
Don't fret the scars, either on the inside or outside
Let your pups grow to be wolves, their fur worn in pride

Bullets

✦ People will go to great lengths to prove their own stupidity

✦ A person's intelligence should not be gauged by the volume of words coming out of their mouth, nor the quality of the words. Even a parrot can be conditioned to say big and complicated words.

✦ "I don't think, therefore I'm not"

What Being A Wolf Means To Me

I have always questioned everything including authority. I cannot point to a single thing that changed that, seems like I was born that way. When you are a young wolf, you question everything and rebel against everything. As you grow older, along with that comes responsibilities, family, job, etc. For a very few, they may end up working for themselves or working in an industry that does not care if they express their wolf-like qualities all the time, as long as they do their work (drilling industry, tattoo shops, etc) but for most of the young wolfs, they end up having to conform to a degree in order to feed families and keep employed. I don't consider that to be a bad thing but a mark of a wolf's adaptability to changing situations, no different than what a wolf in the wild would do.

Depending on the type of work you do or the path in life you choose, the wolf becomes more covert versus overt. If you are a wolf, the sheep will recognize it and fear and possibly either despise or respect you. It may be the look in your eye, your body language or other subtle signals you send off.

What it means to be a wolf, in my opinion, is different for each person with some common ties. It may include all or some of the qualities already posted or none of them. I think trying to describe what a wolf looks like is like trying to describe what yellow looks like to a person that has been blind all their life or what the shape of a cloud is. A true wolf defies description or labels, they may outwardly change with the situation but their mentally and spirit will always remain the same. They can be of any race, sex, sexual orientation, or religion. They may be the fat guy walking down the street or the quadriplegic in the wheel chair. They may be wearing a suit or a black t-shirt.

The sheep are pretty easy to define; the wolves are a bit more difficult to pin down.

Tao Of The Wolf

In this essay, I will endeavor to describe Wolf Tao or "The way of the wolf".

To me, Taoist ethics perfectly describe what it means to be a wolf. And is the direct opposite of what we see in the behavior of the "sheep" or "sheeple" we so often rant about.

There are many variations of the Tao but for the purposes of this essay I'm going to use these 6 ethics.

Selflessness

Moderation

Embracing the Mystery

Non-Contrivance

Detachment

Humility

I will explore each of these ethics in some depth to explain what to me "Wolf Tao" is.

Is there really such thing as a "Wolf Tao"? To me there is but to quote Tao Te Ching:

"How do I know this is true? By looking inside myself."

The purpose of this essay is as much to look inside myself as it is to try to educate or enlighten anyone.

What follows is what to me is the path of being a wolf.

Tao Te Ching (Dào Dé Jīng; ascribed to Laozi) quotes in each chapter are from the R. B. Blakney, Translation, 1955. Listed as public domain

Selflessness

The sky is everlasting
And the earth is very old.
Why so? Because the world
Exists not for itself;
It can and will live on.
The Wise Man chooses to be last
And so becomes the first of all;
Denying self, he too is saved.
For does he not fulfillment find
In being an unselfish man?

- Tao Te Ching, Chapter 7

The sheep are often the greediest of creatures. In the process of following the flock and getting caught into this endless cycle of consumerism, they become totally self-centered. They identity becomes defined by what they have. What they have is dictated by the latest fads or what their friends and family have (other members of the flock). In the pursuit of buying these gadgets, latest fashion and trinkets, they often buy themselves into debt, sometimes into bankruptcy. In the process of buying more and more, they have less and less to give. Often their very family will go wanting because money is used to purchase a new TV or fancy car instead of medical care or education.

But to the sheep this is no big thing and no different than what the other sheep in their flock is doing. The cycle of greed drives the cycle of spending which drives the cycle of debt which drives the cycle of working any and all jobs to keep the cycle going.

The greed is not only in money but time and dedication of self to a cause. The sheep works 14 hour days to feed the cycle and when he gets home he is too exhausted to spend time with his family. There are not enough hours in the day for his family or any type of volunteer work. The sheep, to somewhat assuage the guilt from these, things will donate money to his church and buy more shiny things for his family to compensate for his absence or disinterest.

Contrast this with the wolves that will usually help out others, fellow wolves or sheep, with time or money. Because the wolves are less likely to buy frivolous things, they usually have a bit more money to give and more time to dedicate to family and/or volunteer work. While by modern standards their lives may seem sparse and near poverty levels, they have what they need, and generally provide for their families well.

While the wolf may seem gruff and rough on the outside, he is likely the only one that will stop in the pouring rain to help a lady change a flat tire while the sheep drive on by.

They may be the paramedics, firefighters and law enforcement, working for low pay, that risk their ass to save others' lives.

You may see the wolves in the jungles giving medical care on mission trips or providing aid to people in disaster situations. While the sheep will donate a pittance to their church (who uses 80% of the donation for "administrative" purposes) or to a charity and then the sheep will pat themselves on the back and brag about how generous they are.

Wolves will sacrifice all to protect and provide for their families. The sheep will work themselves to death for a certain lifestyle or conversely, bleat continually for government handouts so they don't have to work. While the wolf may occasionally need the help from others, it is a short-term help that he either pays back directly or helps others in the future as an indirect return for help received.

Moderation

To take all you want
Is never as good
As to stop when you should.
Scheme and be sharp
And you'll not keep it long.
One can never guard
His home when it's full
Of jade and fine gold:
Wealth, power and pride
Bequeath their own doom.
When fame and success
Come to you, then retire.
This is the ordained Way.

- Tao Te Ching, Chapter 9

Moderation is synonymous with self-control. The sheep may have group or flock-control but they have little self control. Almost everything they do is dictated by what the flock does. There lack of self control is one thing that drives them to mass and over consumerism. Keeping up with the flock means only having as much or as little self-control as the other sheep have in the flock.

The wolf on the other hand is very good at self-moderation. In the wild you seldom see a wolf or wolf pack kill more than they can eat. Little goes to waste. Self-control to the wolf is a survival mechanism. Having control over yourself, your emotions, your urges can often mean the difference between survival and death.

In the modern world, the human wolf exercises self-control or moderation to avoid overspending, becoming fat, becoming out of shape.

But the wolf also has to exhibit a great deal of moderation or self-control in order to avoid being assimilated into the flock. You see not exercising self-control or moderation is the easiest thing to do. The wolf chooses the difficult right over the easy wrong and avoids the comfortable trap of not controlling himself lest he wake up one day and his coat is now wool.

Embracing the Mystery

The omnipresent Virtue will take shape
According only to the Way.
The Way itself is like something
Seen in a dream, elusive, evading one.
In it are images, elusive, evading one.
In it are things like shadows in twilight.
In it are essences, subtle but real,
Embedded in truth.
From of old until now,
Under names without end,
The First, the Beginning is seen.
How do I know the beginning of all,
What its nature may be?
By these!

- Tao Te Ching, Chapter 21

The sheep detest mystery and the unknown. The sheepherders realize this and makes sure that the flocks continue towards a direction that keeps the flock docile. To lead them into the unknown would scare the flock and scatter them in panic. That is why that, regardless of the TV channel, you are seeing the same thing. With variations on a theme the news media keeps the message the same and sugarcoats the bad news that might affect the sheep. Bad things that happen outside of the USA is presented in such a way that the sheep feel that their government, the Powers That Be (PTB) are protecting them and keeping them secure so they don't explore any deeper than what is coming out of the television, to do so would be stepping into the unknown. Outside of their homes and offices, they pretty much are the same way. Driving around in climate controlled boxes, wrapped in layers of fashion designer clothes to keep them warm or cool. Exposure to the elements is something they avoid. When you do see them in the sun with much exposed skin, it is slathered in multiple layers of protective chemicals lest they burn. The sheep don't like nature; it is a mystery to them.

The wolves on the other hand love mystery. We can't seem to keep our noses out of dark places both physically and mentally. By this I mean that in the wild, like our 4 legged brothers, the human wolf will be exploring, poking into the caves, seeing what is over the next hill. Experiencing nature in the truest sense.

And in the modern world, we are just as curious. Seeing what is on TV, we are continually digging deeper not believing the propaganda and hype. We are not satisfied with what the talking-heads are saying on the TV until we have explored deeper and convinced ourselves that what they say is true.

Non-Contrivance (receptiveness)

"Govern the realm by the right,
And battles by stratagem."
The world is won by refraining.
How do I know this is so?
By this:
As taboos increase, people grow poorer;
When weapons abound, the state grows chaotic;
Where skills multiply, novelties flourish;
As statutes increase, more criminals start.
So the Wise Man will say:
As I refrain, the people will reform:
Since I like quiet, they will keep order;

When I forebear, the people will prosper;
When I want nothing, they will be honest.

- Tao Te Ching, Chapter 57

The wolves are nothing if not receptive. Wolves will open their homes and lives to people from all races, religions, sex, etc once we accept them as being wolves in spirit. Wolves are always receptive to new ideas even if these ideas challenge our own thinking. Unlike the sheep, we enjoy the challenge to our thinking. Having your thinking challenged either validates your views or forces you to change your views. Like steel is tempered by fire so too is the wolf's thinking tempered by exposure to challenges.

The sheep however are not receptive to anything other than moving as one with the flock to the next fad or protest. They live in constant fear of anything alien to their normal, everyday lives and are not receptive to anything that might disrupt those lives. They are not receptive to mingling with other races or cultures except in a "passing past the monkey cage" fashion, in other words, safe and sound on the other side of the glass (TV screen). Anything that challenges the group-think of the flock is fought against with opinions heard on TV or read on the internet. The sheep are receptive only to information that is careful fed to them by the sheepherders. And that information is carefully vetted before feeding to keep the flock calm.

Detachment

Touch ultimate emptiness,
Hold steady and still.
All things work together:
I have watched them reverting,
And have seen how they flourish
And return again, each to his roots.

This, I say, is the stillness:
A retreat to one's roots;
Or better yet, return
To the will of God,
Which is, I say, to constancy.
The knowledge of constancy
I call enlightenment and say
That not to know it
Is blindness that works evil.
But when you know
What eternally is so,
You have stature
And stature means righteousness
And righteousness is kingly
And kingliness divine
And divinity is the Way
Which is final.
Then, though you die,
You shall not perish.

- Tao Te Ching, Chapter 16

Detachment (or lack of same) for the sheep is difficult. And often is difficult for the wolf as well.

Detachment can mean being detached from the modern world and all its comforts. It can mean being detached from a social group, family and friends. It can mean becoming detached from your adult children when they move out of the home.

It can also mean detachment from life, in other words, death.

In the case of becoming detached from the modern world, the wolf has little difficulty with this since the modern world is based on propaganda, over consumerism and control, all of which the wolf shuns whenever possible. But conversely, these things are

HOWLS FROM THE WOLFPACK

comforting to the sheep and as a result, they are loath to detach from them.

The sheep also do not want to detach from their flock, another source of comfort for the sheep. Often this is a religious group that is controlling but this control is a comfort for the sheep and they do not feel comfortable without this controlling influence in their lives.

The wolves may very well be a member of a religious group but it is one that is usually independent, free thinking and open to exploring and criticizing the dogma of the church. Unfortunately these churches are few in numbers and as a result, wolves are often unaffiliated with a church. Wolves often describe themselves as spiritual not religious. For the wolf, time spent out with nature is a more spiritual experience than spending time in a church.

Both wolves and sheep may have problems with detaching from family, especially when it becomes time for their children to move out when they become adults. The difference is that the wolves have spent many years preparing their pups for adulthood and independence whereas the sheep have only raised their children to become adult sheep who have problems functioning independently. The wolf watches with pride as his pups become independent adults while the sheep constantly second guesses and micromanages the adult child because they were not raised independent.

But perhaps the most important part of detachment is when the days are over for the wolf and the sheep.

The wolf will pass from this world to the next perhaps peacefully, perhaps violently. Either way the wolf will take his final breath knowing that he lived a life well and good. That his memories and accomplishments will be talked about for generations and will benefit of his descendants. His final thoughts will be sad but good. Thoughts of those he is living behind but memories of adventures, battles won and people loved will fill his final moments. The detachment from this life will be hard but accepted as being part of the cycle.

But to the sheep their final moments will be of terror knowing that their lives were no different than millions of carbon copies of themselves. That they have ill prepared their families to carry on after them. That there were opportunities to shed their wool and follow the Tao of the Wolf that they did not take and since they chose not to, their lives will end incomplete and empty. The passing of the sheep will be with a pitiful whimper. The will struggle with detaching from this world in the vain hopes of a few final moments to gain what the wolves have had all their lives. They will know in their final moments that their memories will fade quickly for their descendants and future generations will know little of them because the sheep accomplished little in their lives.

Humility

To those who would help
The ruler of men
By means of the Way:
Let him not with his militant might
Try to conquer the world;
This tactic is like to recoil.
For where armies have marched,
There do briars spring up;
Where great hosts are impressed,
Years of hunger and evil ensue.
The good man's purpose once attained,
He stops at that;
He will not press for victory.
His point once made, he does not boast,
Or celebrate the goal he gained,
Or proudly indicate the spoils.
He won the day because he must:

But not by force or violence.
That things with age decline in strength,
You well may say, suits not the Way;
And not to suit the Way is early death.

- Tao Te Ching, Chapter 30

The wolf is one of the strongest and fastest creatures in some parts of the world. Their cunning and speed is the stuff that the Native Americans sang about. But with that comes humility. By this I mean that a wolf would never hunt more than it could eat or kill an animal just for the sake of killing. Only humans seem to do this. But the human wolf is much the same way. While we may be very strong, very brave, good with guns, black belts, whatever, we have achieved these things to better ourselves, not to hold over others. If we hunt, we hunt to eat wasting little of the kill. We might display some trophy of the kill but as much as anything else, it is in respect to the animal we killed. A wolf of two legs is very similar to one of 4 legs. We might seem placid and at home in the wild and we accept nature and our own ways with a degree of humility but if you cross us, we will destroy you. We just won't brag about it (much) later.

The sheep on the other hand, any humility they have is a survival mechanism brought on by their weakness. But usually they puff out their chest and boast of their latest purchase and being some sort of personal accomplishment.

Conclusion

If these 6 ethics of the Wolf Tao seem simple it is because, well, they are. Like moves in a game of chess, learning the principals of the Tao are simple but mastery will never come to any of us. But like any journey, the path or Tao to being a wolf is the adventure.

If there was an end point, besides death, some point where we could claim some sort of victory or prize, I suspect the wolves would be disappointed. Likely we would stop short of receiving the prize and return back to the beginning along a different path if that was possible, and begin our journey anew.

The Tao or path to being a wolf is different for each person. Each member of the pack might have a different description of these 6 ethics and that is fine. Like a journey to the mountaintop, there are multiple paths that reach the same destination. The path you take is not as important as the journey itself. Some paths will be easy, some hard but they ultimately reach the same goal.

Finally one symbol of Tao is the Yin-Yang. A lot of westerners consider this to mean good and evil but that is not correct. The Yin and the Yang are separate and equal qualities that represent the good and the bad, birth and death, men and women. A wolf understands that life is about balance. That you have to control both the good and the bad within you.

Perhaps a better description lies in an old Cherokee legend:

An old Cherokee is teaching his grandson about life. "A fight is going on inside me," he said to the boy.

"It is a terrible fight and it is between two wolves. One is evil - he is anger, envy, sorrow, regret, greed, arrogance, self-pity, guilt, resentment, inferiority, lies, false pride, superiority, and ego." He continued, "The other is good - he is joy, peace, love, hope, serenity, humility, kindness, benevolence, empathy, generosity, truth, compassion, and faith. The same fight is going on inside you - and inside every other person, too."

The grandson thought about it for a minute and then asked his grandfather, "Which wolf will win?"

The old Cherokee simply replied, "The one you feed."

Hardcore Mind

When you look at the elite, be them Navy SEALS, ultra-marathon runners, successful businessmen (or women), missionaries living in the middle of Africa caring for the locals or Tibetan monks living on top of a snowy mountaintop, they all seem to have one thing in common. Mental toughness, strong willed, or as I call it, a "hardcore mind".

There used to be a t-shirt that said "your brain is your primary weapon" I prefer to say that your brain is your primary tool (weapons are also tools, not all tools are weapons). Your "tool" may be the computer, a set of wrenches, commercial kitchen or a fighter jet but all of them are completely and utterly worthless without a set of human hands to operate them. Those hands are commanded in what they do by your brain or mind. If your mind is not focused or disciplined enough, you do not do your job, or at least you don't do it well.

Chairman Mao once said: "Civilize the mind but make savage the body". While I understand what he is saying, I would argue that in order to "make savage the body", you have to preserve and cultivate the savage part of our mind.

Our brains are wired to do this; it is part of the primal that still resides in us all. But over the centuries, as we have gotten more and more "civilized", we have lost touch with our primal side. When it comes to survival, regardless of if it is in the wild hunting for food or in the boardroom fighting for an idea, that primal part of us needs to be cultivated and ready to be tapped.

That primal part of our brain is our "hardcore mind".

There is a lot of talk about developing a hardcore mind in athletics and the military but to me this is too narrow a focus.

While you no doubt need a tight focus to get thru SEAL training or to run a marathon, this hardcore mind development is built around these particular task or groups. So to someone that does not desire to be a Navy SEAL or run a 100 mile ultra, they often think they have no need for developing a hardcore mind. And if you are content to continue being one of the flocks then you are right, you really don't need to get mentally hardcore. It takes little thinking or discipline to follow the ass of the sheep in front of you.

However, if your goal is more than following the flock over the cliff's edge into the abyss, then you have to change your way of thinking. You have to get mentally tough. You have to develop a hardcore mind.

Now be warned, this is nothing that happens overnight. As a matter of fact, you will never reach the ultimate level of having a hardcore mind but rest assured, as you go forward developing the most important muscle in your body, your brain, (and yes, I know the brain is not a muscle, you know what I'm talking about), your life will become more successful. If you goal is a hardcore body, it starts with a hardcore mind. If your goal is to become rich, getting hardcore about achieving this goal is the start.

Achieving lofty goals starts with developing a hardcore mind.

This path towards a hardcore mind for me started when I began working ambulances. Your mental focus and toughness would make the difference between your patient living or dying. If the call was difficult, if your patient was melded in amongst 2 tons of twisted automotive metal, you couldn't say "fuck this, too difficult, lets go for coffee", you had to stay focused. It might be 105 degrees or -20 and snowing. Failure was not an option. I spent the better part of 20 years doing this type of work not only in the US but overseas in 3rd world countries.

Having a critical patient 10 minutes from the hospital is nothing compared to having a critical patient 10 miles off the coast of India with no helicopter support. Often the only medically trained person on the offshore construction barge, my mental focus had to be laser precise when needed and I had to be able to switch it on out of a dead sleep if someone was hurt, I was on call 24/7. When you work in those conditions, you become pretty hardcore.

Getting to this point of being hardcore was nothing I was trained to do beyond my medical training. There are no courses that I know of on how to develop a hardcore mind but your job training and experience might help you develop that mentality. In the pre-hospital emergency medicine field, you either get hardcore or you get out. The same can be said of being a firefighter or in law enforcement.

But I'm developing a hardcore mind (remember, it is a journey you never really reach the end of) by happenstance more so that by planning. So reflecting back on that, I decided to put together a bit of a blueprint to developing a hardcore mind.

A hardcore mind can be seen in the corporate boardroom and in the cancer wards. In the battlefield and on the baseball field. In the classroom and in the boxing ring. Developing a hardcore mind has nothing to do with being male or female, your race, sexual orientation, job or body type. It has everything to do with what is between your ears and how you use it.

"Some Warriors look fierce, but are mild. Some seem timid, but are vicious. Look beyond appearances; position yourself for the advantage.
- **Deng Ming-Dao**

"Strength does not come from physical capacity. It comes from an indomitable will." **Mohandas Gandhi**

Developing a hardcore mind may be done by different people in different ways but to me what follows are the steps to developing a hardcore mind. I'll explain each one more in depth later on in this essay.

1. **Situational awareness**
2. **Get comfortable with being uncomfortable**
3. **Be prepared**
4. **Adaptability**
5. **Put others first**
6. **Control your emotions externally**
7. **Think outside of the box**
8. **Have a goal and break it down**
9. **Never be afraid of failing (and stop bitching when you do)**
10. **Disregard the previous 9 steps**

Now a bit of a disclaimer here, if in the following paragraphs I suggest something physical as an exercise to developing a hardcore mind, use your head and don't kill or injure yourself. If you have a medical condition, get a doctor's clearance before doing anything such as fasting or anything else I suggest that might cause you harm or exacerbate an existing condition. In other words, use a bit of common sense.

Situational awareness or SA

The term Situational Awareness was first used by fighter pilots to describe a state of constant awareness of the environment around them and their place in that environment. At the speed with which flight operations occur, being oblivious to your surroundings is a recipe for a quick death. It has since been adapted and used to describe the constantly changing environment in military and police operations.

Situational Awareness or SA can be extended beyond combat and air operations. It can be used to not only give you a "heads up" to threats but also to opportunities. Most people walk around in a complete and oblivious state to what is happening around them. Not only do they miss potential threats but they also miss out on a lot of good things, including opportunities.

The best way that I have heard SA put was by colors:

White

Totally oblivious to your surroundings. Potential cues to the senses are missed completely or only are noticed once they increase in size. An example of being in a white state of SA would be sitting at home, watching TV with your family. Not a bad state to be in given the environment but most people never leave that state except to go direct to the black level.

Yellow

Your senses are open and receiving. There is no direct threat but your mental radar is on continuous scan for threats, or opportunities. An example would be leaving your home (safe environment) and getting in your car to drive to work. Eyes scanning, ears listening, all senses working to the highest potential.

Orange

While in your state of yellow SA, something has shown up on your mental radar. It might be a sound that should not be there, a slight vibration in the steering wheel of your car, something seen out of the corner of your eye or a smell that should not be there. You scan until you find the source of blip on your radar, if nothing threatening; you go back into yellow SA. Until deemed a non-threat, you are mentally preplanning looking for escape routes, defensive measures, etc. Think the slight smell of smoke in a movie theater.

Red

The blip on your mental radar is a threat and since you are mentally prepared for it, you put your preplanning into play. You are moving towards the emergency exit before the people stuck in white SA know what is happening. You are moving away from the moving shadow you saw in the alley entrance and ready to defend yourself. If you are carrying a weapon, it is out and ready to be used.

Black

This is total panic and results from being in the white (oblivious) SA state and being thrown directly into a bad situation without going through the previous levels. This is also called the brown state because at this point, people often dump the contents of their bowels into their underwear.

So how does SA play into developing a hardcore mind? For one, it is a constant exercise that you can go through. When you drive, when you walk through the mall, you constantly scan around you looking for potential threats. This can be a car in front of you with a wobbly tire that the driver does not know about. It could be the body language of the person approaching you on the street. It could be that faint smell of something when you come home that turns out to be a gas leak.

Once you get used to doing this constant scan, once your mental radar is continuously on, it becomes second nature. The things that you pickup on may be pretty mundane but easily avoided. How many people have you known that fell because they were not watching where they were going? Ever had something that tugged at your "sixth sense" that you ignored and turned out to be a problem? This was likely visual, audio or other cues you missed.

With your mental radar scanning, it becomes a subconscious exercise and you will find that you start reacting to a threat before you consciously realize the threat is there.

But this also transfers into everyday life in that you become more aware of what is around you, the good and the bad. You might find that business opportunities become more apparent, you see small clues to potential big problems and not to seem trite, but you actually do stop to smell the roses.

Don't walk around clueless, don't get caught in the white SA, stay in yellow when you walk out of your house. Take in the clues of both good and bad things in your world. Use all of your senses: sight, hearing, smell, touch & taste. These together, when working and scanning, are what make up the legendary "6th sense" that you hear about. Cultivate it and use it.

Get comfortable with being uncomfortable

"Be careful in dealing with a man who cares nothing for comfort or promotion, but is simply determined to do what he believes to be right. He is a dangerous uncomfortable enemy, because his body, which you can always conquer, gives you little purchase upon his soul."
- Gilbert Murray

We become weak, in mind and body, when we become too comfortable and when we fail to face our fears.

Let me give you a couple of personal examples.

Back in the 80s, I took a break from being in emergency medical services and became a Deputy Sheriff. I had been a reserve deputy for a while and decided to try it full-time. Most of my time was spent in maximum security but I also decided to join the tactical team. I loved it! Lots of guns, shooting with someone else paying the tab, new gadgets to play with, etc. Then the day came when they decided that we need to learn to rappel. Now while my fear of heights was not what I would call a phobia, I did have a healthy respect of heights and would get a knot in my belly when I was up on a ladder. Our first lesson was off the new jail building which was about 15 feet tall. Up on the roof, tied off on the line, stand on the edge and back off. Scared the shit out of me! But when I hit the ground, I was ready to do it again. An all day affair that I really got into.

But then the next day of training, 15 feet was replaced with about 80 feet, off the old jail. Not only off the top but on the roof you had to get on a ladder, climb on top of the wall, hook up and swing over, then down. Hardest thing I have ever done in my life! But once I hit the ground, I was hooked and back up to do it several more times. Exposure to doing something "uncomfortable" made me comfortable (but still respectful) of heights.

Another personal example is that over the last 16 years, most of my work has been overseas, usually in 3rd world countries. When practical, I have shunned hotel rooms and tried to live more out in the communities taking part in as much as their culture as I could. This has been in places like Nigeria, Egypt, Yemen and Kazakhstan, among others. To say that I was put into some uncomfortable (and scary) circumstances would be an understatement but the wealth of experiences, knowledge and development of a hardcore mind cannot be overstated.

By being comfortable with being uncomfortable, by facing your fears, you will further develop your hardcore mind. People with phobias have been "cured" by repeated exposure to what their phobia was about. A success rate reported as 90% by David Barlow, director of Boston University's Center for Anxiety and Related Disorders.

Pick what makes you uncomfortable and confront it. One major fear that people have is over public speaking. Consider joining a public speaking group near you and polish your public speaking skills. On the physical side, try making yourself uncomfortable by fasting. I regularly fast for up to 48 hours straight; good source of willpower (but remember my disclaimer before attempting this yourself). I also go barefoot a good bit of the time which is not only better for me but increases my situational awareness, you pay more attention where your walking when you don't have shoes on.

The things our body and mind can adapt to are endless if we but put ourselves out there and get comfortable with being uncomfortable.

Part of being comfortable with being uncomfortable is living minimally. When you think about it, much of what we think of as needing to be "comfortable" is defined by the corporations, our culture, the TV, movies, etc. In a space of a few thousand years, we have evolved in a cultural sense but our bodies are designed to function pretty much the same now as millions of years ago (or thousands or whatever, depending on who you believe).

Things that we take for granted now as needing to be comfortable were alien to people even a hundred years ago. Air conditioning, cars, AC in cars, satellite TV systems, mobile phones, these are things that we take for granted now but up until a few decades ago, nobody had more than 3-4 channels on the TV. Color TV was expensive and uncommon. Mobile phones were unheard of. AC in the house was maybe an evaporative unit, if any.

We were raised without these things and didn't miss them because we didn't know what we were missing. Now these things are a "must have". Can you imagine anyone in Texas buying a house or car without AC? How many people panic when they get 3 miles from the house and realize that they have forgotten their mobile phone?

Don't get me wrong, these things are nice and yes, I have all of those things but they get little use. My mobile phone is a company requirement that I carry the thing but it gets little use. My car has AC and I do use it on the hottest days (at the time of this writing, I'm living in Egypt). I have a satellite TV that came with my apartment that I watch on occasion. But if all these things were taken away tomorrow, I would survive and likely get more done without the distractions.

Getting used to doing without "stuff" is getting comfortable with being uncomfortable. I have found that the less I own, the less I need.

Be prepared

When the World is at Peace, a gentleman keeps his Sword by his side."
- Wu Tsu

Being prepared applies to physical and mental preparation. Any survival situation is more dependent on being mentally prepared than being physically prepared. However, being physically prepared for not only survival situations but also day-to-day life has an impact on your attitude.

If you are fat and out of shape, your chances of survival are less than if you are fit regardless of how mentally prepared you are.

Being physically fit helps you daily in the mundane things also. It increases your confidence levels, gives you a more aggressive body language.

Being prepared materially gives you confidence for unforeseen circumstances. Having the tools to survive, other than your mind, enables you survive but enables you to help others if you, yourself, are not a victim of whatever has happened.

Some simple examples are what do you EDC or Every Day

Carry? Do you always keep a flashlight, knife and lighter with you? Simple things until the need arise for them. For me, on my person, I always have at least one knife, a small high-intensity flashlight, a multi-tool, lighter, additional knife on a necklace with a spare house key, cell phone, bandanna, the usual watch, wallet, etc. At some point during the week, most of these things come in handy. Every few months, they become critical. This does not count what I carry in my BOB (Bug Out Bag) that stays with me all the time when traveling.

How often have you seen a movie where the characters died or suffered greatly due to just not having a flashlight? Or a knife? Granted their troubles were written into the script but have you ever had a flat tire at night and not had a flashlight to help you fix it? Ever needed to open a box and hunted around for a kitchen knife to cut the tape? Every had a minor problem with your car that could be fixed with a screwdriver but you didn't have a tool kit in your car?

Now some people carry preparedness to a ridiculous level. There are people that spend many thousands of dollars on knives, gadgets, etc. When the go out, the look like they have a bat-belt on. And if this floats your boat, go for it. But your physical preparedness should be based on a few simple guidelines. Your type of work, your ability to use the items, potential threats and your budget.

If you're a cubicle dweller, your EDC needs are not the same as a firefighter. If you can't hit the broadside of a barn with a gun, might not be a good idea to carry one. Your potential threats in Podunk, Texas are not the same as downtown Los Angeles. And if you are on a tight budget, on a daily basis a $30 knife will likely serve your purposes.

Think of it this way, Target, Weapons and Movement.

The target or goal dictates the weapon, tools, knowledge, etc that you need. The target may be a goal; it may be a potential or actual threat.

Once you determine the target then you prepare the weapons or tools that you need to have to achieve or defeat that target/goal. This may be physical fitness needed, tools, skills or actual weapons.

Movement is whatever you need to get into position to use those weapons or tools.

Your target is something that I'll get into under goal setting.

The key to survival is being prepared mentally more so than physically but don't underestimate the need for being physically prepared for day to day life and potential threats.

Adaptability

"JIU YOKU GO O SEI SURU - Flexibility Masters Hardness"

"The day I stop learning is the day they bury me" – Me

How many times have you heard someone say "It ain't my job"? Or had to call in someone to do a simple repair around the house or office. Know anyone that can't change a tire?

There are things in this world that you can only learn to adapt to by constant exposure. If you spend all your days in air conditioning and walk outside in the 100 degree heat, you will start to melt (so it seems). If you spend all day working in the 100 degree heat and go into an air conditioned office, you feel like you are going to freeze. The human body, and mind, has an amazing ability to adapt to its environment. Read about what some of the runners do to prepare for the heat of an ultramarathon.

Look at the training elite military groups do to train for extreme environments.

Ultimately you want to get to the point where you thrive on chaos. To see examples of people that do this on a daily basis, you don't have to look much further than firefighters or paramedics. Their days are filled with sitting in a chair having lunch one minute and the next being thrown into a major trauma call or fully involved structure fire. And speaking for myself, I loved it. I do thrive on chaos. The worse the weather, the more chaotic the situation, the better I function.

But we didn't start off this way. We came to that point by realistic training, experience working but I think the ones of us that stayed in that field for any length of time had the ability to adapt to any situation.

For yourself, you can gain a high degree of adaptability by constantly exposing yourself to situations that are unfamiliar to you. This is also tied to the "getting comfortable with being uncomfortable" part of this essay.

If you go camping, does your car look like a family is migrating across the desert or can you camp with what is on your back and in a small pack because you adapt to make up for all the modern, high tech stuff that you can buy at the store?

At work, do you take on jobs that are outside of your job description? Doing so will help you adapt and learn more, integrate your job with other departments and impress the hell out of your supervisor (job security). It will give you new skills so that if your job ends, you can adapt and move on to another job.

Never stop learning, never stop adapting, and never stop evolving in your life.

<u>Put others first</u>

"Laws control the lesser man. Right conduct controls the greater one." ~Chinese Proverb

"Do the difficult right instead of the easy wrong" Unknown

"Victory goes to the one who has no thought of himself."- Shinkage School of Swordsmanship

This can mean putting your family first, your team first or your company first. It means carrying little about the cost to yourself to accomplish your goals which may be personal goals. Now I don't mean that you work yourself into an early grave for your employer or that you kill yourself in order to lose a few pounds. That is not what I'm talking about here.

When you take an honest look at your vices, your weaknesses, I'm pretty sure that you will find out that they are pretty selfish.

The things that most of us do that ends up destroying our health, families, jobs, etc are usually pretty selfish. In order to reach long term goals, you often have to make short term sacrifices to yourself. In order to get in better physical condition, you have to sacrifice that cake you really love or not sit around in the comfy chair all day watching football.

By making these personal sacrifices, we move towards our goals or targets for ourselves and our families. We become better spouses, parents or employees. We become better businessmen.

Making these personal sacrifices takes willpower, a hardcore mind. Pick one of your vices and knock it down. No whining, just determination to be better and not bitch about the sacrifice that it takes to be better. Pick something small and squash it. Build on success and move on to something larger.

The day will come when you will make your choices, not based on short-term comfort or satisfaction but on long term goals and what you need to obtain those goals. It will become second nature and by having made personal sacrifices to obtain those goals, you will have made strides towards developing a hardcore mind.

Control your emotions externally

"The way I have chosen is one of discipline. It requires me to overcome my sentiments, lead a stoic life, immerse myself in hardship. If I don't, the light I seek will escape me"-Unknown

"Mental bearing (calmness), not skill, is the sign of a matured samurai. A Samurai therefore should neither be pompous nor arrogant." - Tsukahara Bokuden

This also pertains to internally controlling your emotions.

Often this is a difficult thing to do but if you can remain calm, inside and out, then you make decisions based on rational thought instead of raw emotion.

Now don't get me wrong, there is a time and place for honest emotion. There is nothing wrong with a man laughing at something funny his child does or crying at a funeral. But your emotions should run deep and let loose when they serve you best or at appropriate times.

To use paramedics again as an example (give me a break, I am one, it is what I know), paramedics see human tragedy on a daily basis. Dead or dying kids, families finding grandpa dead in the bed in the morning, happy families destroyed in a split second by a drunk driver, etc. Most paramedics see more tragedy in a single day that most other people will see in a decade. When you are working a cardiac arrest on a child, the tragedy of the moment is something you just can't dwell on. Given into your emotions at that point will cloud your judgment and weaken your skills. If you have to breakdown due to a call, you do it after the call in a safe environment; most of us went out to get something to eat afterwards.

Emotions while okay given the right circumstances, can be detrimental in others.

In the business world, how many times have you heard about someone that destroyed their job or ruined a relationship because of an email sent in the heat of emotions? How many people buy stuff or eat shitty food because they are buying or eating emotionally?

Now a bit of disclaimer here: for the most part, I consider 90% of the so called "emotional disorders" and various syndromes that the mental health profession has come up with to be complete and utter bullshit. That being said, if you have a problem you can't control, get help for it.

So how do you exercise self restraint over emotions? Think before you talk, or don't talk at all unless you have something worthwhile to say. Walk away from the computer before pushing the send button on an email that might get you fired or damage a relationship. Be humble in victory, apologize when you screw up, and learn from your mistakes.

If you cannot control your emotions internally, try not to show them externally. Always appear confident and ready for action. Easier said than done? Perhaps but start, start somewhere. Don't rise to the bait when someone at work tries to push your buttons. Don't give them the satisfaction of seeing you externally expressing the rage you are feeling inside. Don't let them control your responses.

Don't let bad emotions rising from a bad relationship destroy you. Work on fixing the relationship or end it and move on.

Don't sweat the small stuff and most of the things we get upset about are small stuff.

Think outside of the box

"The individual has always had to struggle to keep from being overwhelmed by the tribe. If you try it, you will be lonely often, and sometimes frightened. But no price is too high to pay for the privilege of owning yourself." -- **Friedrich Nietzsche**

"I have been thinking so far outside of the box for so long, I have forgotten where the damn thing is." **Me**

Every great stride that mankind has made came from thinking outside of the box. If people had followed whatever conventional thinking was at the time, we would have no space program, developed new technology or left the ground to fly in airplanes. The phone would not have been discovered nor would most other things we took for granted. What we think of as "thinking outside of the box" used to be called visionary. This is a trait that it critical to developing a hardcore mind.

Regardless of if we are talking about starting a business or reacting to an emergency situation (fire in your house, etc), you have to be able to think outside of the box and constantly reassess your thinking.

Responding to an emergency, fighting a fire, building a business or raising a family all require unconventional thinking in order to be successful.

To help develop this trait, constantly think "what if?" as you go through the day. As your driving down the road and see a truck in front of you, think "what if it jackknives?" how will you respond? "What if" your house catches on fire or someone tries to break in a night while you are home? If you are starting a business, "What if" your service or product becomes obsolete? The possibilities are endless as are the scenarios but doing this constantly will do several things: a) you will start developing more flexibility in your thinking b) you will raise your situational awareness c) you may pickup on potential problems and head them off, or mitigate the effects.

Remember that the box gets bigger daily. More and more people do nothing on a daily basis but think inside of the box. If you ever want to rise above the average Joe, if you ever want to free yourself of the flock of sheep you are part of, you have to start thinking outside of the box.

Have a goal and break it down

Take heed you do not find what you do not seek. **English proverb**

For the cynical:

"Goals are important, how will we know how much we have failed if we don't set a goal in the first place" **Me**

Goals are important, breaking your goals down into manageable targets more so. If your goal is to climb Mount Everest, go for it but to achieve that goal, you will have to break down the attainment of that goal into manageable steps.

The goal of winning wars is to defeat your enemies. This may be a war waged by a nation or a personal war against an addiction. Regardless, winning the war is the goal but that goal is reached by multiple battles. Each battle is won, or lost, after preparation for each battle. The more you prepare, the greater your chances for success. The more realistically you train and prepare, the more likely you are to when each battle and ultimately, the war. The loss of a single battle does not mean you have lost the war but it is an opportunity to analyze what you did wrong, and right, correct and move on to the next battle.

Look at your goal as your personal war. Define your goal and each battle needed to win that war. Prepare for each battle, win or lose, analyze what went wrong and right and move on.

Don't allow a single defeat to derail your campaign to win your personal war.

The simplest way that I have heard to setup goals or targets with the greatest chance of success is using the acronym ACTE which stands for:

Assess the situation
Create a simple plan
Take action
Evaluate your progress

If your goal is large, you might have to use the ACTE tool with each smaller goal or battle that you are waging in order to win the war.

Never be afraid of failing (and don't bitch when you do)

"It is defeat," says **Henry Ward Beecher**, "that turns bone to flint, and gristle to muscle, and makes men invincible, and formed those heroic natures that are now in ascendancy in the world. Do not, then, be afraid of defeat. You are never so near to victory as when defeated in a good cause."

"It does not matter how slowly you go so long as you do not stop."
– Confucius

"If you know the enemy and know yourself you need not fear the results of a hundred battles." - **Sun Tzu**

History is full of heroes: successful business men, mighty warriors, great statesmen, healing doctors, groundbreaking scientist, etc, the one common denominator between all of them is that they failed at some point in their lives, many times.

What separates these denizens of history from the forgotten is that they are remembered for their successes which they never would have had if they had not continued to move forward after they had failed. History forgotten is full of people that failed but never moved past their failures to success.

One of the first steps in moving forward after failure is to recognize it as a learning experience. Evaluate what you did right and wrong, repeat what you did right, correct what you did wrong and move on.

And for god's sake, don't fucking whine about it all the time! Perhaps someone or something was an influence in your failure. Business failure because of poor economy, weight loss failure because of (supposed) food addictions, whatever but stop shifting blame from your own failures onto somebody, or something else. Recognize these things as being factors in your failure, i.e., abundance of fast-food places in your neighborhood but it was not the fast-food places fault that you chose to stop there and spend YOUR money on their crappy food. It was a CHOICE you made.

There is one fitness guru that said that if you wanted to succeed in your diet, first off throw out all the crappy food you had in your house. Well, duh! If you're an alcoholic, throw out the booze and don't go to bars. If you don't want to eat shitty food, throw it out of your house regardless of what you paid for it.

While failure is part of living, remove obstacles that might cause needless failure. Some failures are a result of things outside of your control, deal with these and move on. But the things that might cause you to fail that you can control, control them! Pretty simple right?

Disregard the previous 9 steps

"Ultimately, you must forget about technique. The further you progress, the fewer teachings there are. The Great Path is really NO PATH." - **Ueshiba Morihei**

Ultimately each of us wolves has found our own path to development of a hardcore mind. We have each found a way to face our own fears and defeat them or at least become comfortable with them. If the previous 9 steps help you towards developing your own hardcore mind, great, if not for you, then forge your own path. In the end, the path you blaze yourself will benefit you more than the one that someone takes you by the hand and leads you down.

Often the steps to developing a hardcore mind will depend on your own strengths and weaknesses.

What is one of your steps today may change a year from now due to your winning that battle.

Conclusion

So there are many people more qualified (at least in their own minds) to write about this subject of developing a hardcore mind, why listen to me? Fair question.

I'll be the first to admit that there are many people out there, Navy SEALS, elite athletes, etc that have written many very good books about developing mental toughness. And I have read most of them but most of them have written from lessons they have learned after many years fighting in wars or competition. I would like to think that I'm coming from a bit more common background that the non-elites might not have and that my words will ring true with those that, like me, have not had the honor of being in those types of groups.

The things that I write are something that anyone regardless of their background can use. And I hope, will have some small measure of impact on their life.

Finally remember that life is hard, Mother Nature is a bitch. Surviving life will not come to any of us. We all die, how we live is important as that is the only part of the cycle we control. Living this life well depends on having a hardcore mind. Determine to live hardcore to achieve your goals, die hardcore to live a legacy behind that your ancestors will remember.

Or stay stuck in your soft-core way of thinking; follow the flock and leaving nothing but quickly fading memories behind.

The choice is yours to make.

I will continue to follow my own path to a hardcore mind. Feel free to follow me on my blog: www.hardcoremind.com to see how I progress, give comments, your own success stories, etc. Or email me at randal@hardcoremind.com.

Until then, stay hardcore!

Randal
April 2011
Egypt
"Make savage the body, but first, make hardcore the mind" Me

Cultural Chaos

For the purposes of this essay, I'm using this definition of culture from the online dictionary

cul·ture

"a : the integrated pattern of human knowledge, belief, and behavior that depends upon the capacity for learning and transmitting knowledge to succeeding generations

b : the customary beliefs, social forms, and material traits of a racial, religious, or social group; also : the characteristic features of everyday existence (as diversions or a way of life} shared by people in a place or time <popular culture> <southern culture>"

Historically major cultures have had little change when you look over their lifespan. There would have been minor changes, perhaps a new but minor invention, etc but overall, the culture stayed on the same path, more or less.

It is easier to think of a culture's direction as points on the compass with North being the direction the culture is going. Over the course of a century or so, their course may swing a degree or two off due north but they are generally headed north.

There are times of major changes of course, the birth of the Guttenberg printing press, the agriculture age starting, the industrial age but even these major changes were gradual taking place over 10s or hundreds of years.

But today these major changes are coming more frequently and from multiple directions. It may be technological, medical, political, etc and they may come all at one time. This creates a cultural chaos that the USA seems to be suffering from.

Now no doubt other countries are going through these changes but most other countries have a more deeply embedded culture that is several hundreds, if not thousands of years old that slow down the changes in the course on their cultural compass. Japan being one example of this, while they are truly leaders in technology, they still maintain a deeply embedded way of thinking that they apply to everything, including business. Their cultural compass is still changing course but doing it slower than ours which gives their people time to gradually assimilate the changes and fit those changes into their centuries old culture.

In the overall history of the world, the USA is a pretty young country and as with most developing country, it took a while before we really had what you would call a culture in place. This was partly due to being a young country and developing and was also due to our country mainly being made up of immigrants who brought their own culture with them.

So now, since we don't have a deeply embedded culture like Japan, our culture compass changes course much quicker and more erratically which creates a type of cultural chaos.

Now chaos can be good sometimes, especially for the Powers That Be. The PTB can use this chaos to keep the citizens off balance and confused. During this confusion, they can pass new laws and controls. Corporations can introduce new products and services that will appear to help relieve some of this chaos.

The people that are affected the most by this chaos are the sheep. The sheepherders use the chaos to help direct and control the flock. The sheep's cultural compass' needle is swinging erratically like multiple magnets of various strengths are trying to pull the needle in many directions at one time. Equate the magnets to the control dogs of the shepherds and you can see how this chaotic influence can be used to control the sheep. Like moving magnets, the yapping dogs, under the shepherd's direction, move the sheep's culture back and forth and the sheep move with this influence.

I think the beginning of this chaos, and the beginning of changing a large percentage of our population from wolves to sheep, is with the introduction of electronic media. The first of these were radio and movies. These were really the first methods of nationwide, or worldwide, advertising. These were more subtle than what we have now but no doubt, it was still a useful tool of the PTB. During both World Wars, movies and radio were used to not only keep the public informed of the war efforts but also used as propaganda tools by the government.

When TV became widespread, this was a major leap forward in a conduit for information to be controlled and disseminated to the public. And it was a powerful tool when there were only 3 major networks that could be controlled by major corporations and the government. The corporations, through paying for advertisement and the government, through control of the airways (FCC) and through control of access of the news media to the White House.

As a result of this control, the PTB could, to a large extent, control what was shown on TV, and perhaps more importantly, what was not shown.

This was a huge shift in our cultural compass but as huge as it was, it was a steady shift. The compass may have shifted from 360 degrees to 90 or more but it pretty much hung steady once that shift happened. The PTB had control of the public because the public was locked into the influence of TV and other electronic media of the time and the PTB pretty much controlled all of these conduits of information.

I think when the cultural chaos started was, to a smaller degree, with cable TV. Suddenly there were more choices which forced the PTB to spread their influence and control to more channels but while this caused the cultural compass needle to shake a bit, once they had control, it steadied out.

The major problem for the PTB was the Internet. Suddenly the exclusive ability to broadcast news worldwide was no longer under the control of the major corporations and government. Anybody could put up a website and become an instant news source. The sheep, because they had already been lured into a false reality of believing whatever came out of the TV, embraced this new source of information as being all true, all the time. This was when our cultural compass went wild.

Because the sheep believed everything to be true that came off the internet, they started getting conflicting information about what they had thought to be true from their years of programming through the TV. In the 1960s, what the sheep believed to be true about the Viet Nam war was controlled by what they saw on TV and in the movies. There were trickles of information about the war that ran contrary to what they saw on TV but due to lack of an ability to get this information out to a large percentage of the population, it didn't spread very far

But seemingly overnight, this information that ran contrary to common belief could be spread not to a small percentage of the US in weeks but throughout the world in minutes or even seconds. It was no longer a matter of coming out in a small distribution newspaper in a few days or in a letter sent to a mailbox but broadcast throughout the world via the Internet to someone on their Smartphone while standing in an elevator.

And the cultural compass went wild! Needle rocking back and forth on sometimes a daily basis. The needle might have only shifted a degree in a week's time but this was the same degree of shift that would happen over a years time 100 years ago and the flock could not handle these constant shifts.

Hence the cultural chaos.

Now the wolves, because they used the ability to think for themselves and see through the bullshit, were not as affected by this chaos and to an extent, even thrived on chaos deep down inside, enjoyed these constant shifts in our culture. But to the flock, the dogs of the shepherds were going crazy, running around the edges of the flock barking out orders that appeared to be conflicting and random driving the sheep back and forth, seemingly without any direction at all.

And that was what the PTB wanted, the sheep off balance, confused, scared. The culture of the flock had changed from one of quiet acceptance of the information from the TV to a culture of constant bombardment of information from multiple sources that kept them off balance, scared and as a result, compliant.

The wolves exploited this new ability to explore deeper into this new cyber world, gather more information and pick the truth from the lies and also used it as a new way of getting out their own message.

The sheep, because they were blinded by their confusion and fear, largely ignored the message of the wolves and continued to be controlled and directed. The sheep, gullible things that they are, accepted everything that came from the major news media, corporations and government as being true and thus, were completely controlled by this media.

The PTB continued to use cultural chaos on the sheep to control them. Don't mistake chaos as always being bad in appearance. A large birthday party for a 5 year old is chaos but a good sort. The PTB used the continuous barrage of information to keep the sheep off balance, to keep the sheep chaotic. The sheep often didn't recognize this as being chaos but as a good thing that our world is changing so fast and for the better. Because they believed it to be good, they accepted it, made it part of themselves giving the PTB control since it was something that the PTB could take away if the sheep did not do as the PTB wished.

The negative chaos was also embraced by the sheep. Chaos created by a terrorist attack, bad economics or potential disease outbreak gave the sheep something to be scared of, which deep down seems to be something they need. As a result of this fear, they willingly gave up freedoms for security from the PTB.

So why do the sheep do this? It appears that they want to be controlled; they want to be coddled and taken care of by the PTB. Much like a baby is happiest when he is secure in his mother's arms and warm, the sheep are happiest when their lives are free from danger (real or not), fat and comfortable. Their happiness is nothing more than a result of their programming by the PTB through the various and numerous input devices (TV, internet, etc) but more of a perceived happiness.

The cultural chaos will continue, at least for the sheep. I don't think the wolves see it as chaos but as challenges to be defeated, battles to be fought. One man's chaos is another man's challenge.

Also, I suppose chaos is relative. To a firefighter the unpredictability of a full involved fire is something he thrives on, as chaotic as it might be it is something he understands and knows how to fight it. To the uninitiated, it is pure, terrifying chaos that they run away from. One man's chaos is another man's challenge.

Anxiety As A Control Mechanism For The Sheeple

From a online encyclopedia:

"Fear is an emotional response to a perceived threat. It is a basic survival mechanism occurring in response to a specific stimulus, such as pain or the threat of danger."

"Fear should be distinguished from the related emotional state of anxiety, which typically occurs without any external threat. "

So from this definition, fear is a legitimate response to a specific stimuli, i.e., you are in a building that is on fire and you fear you will not get out alive, fear you will die, fear you will get burned, all legitimate fears considering the circumstances. If my child has been in a bad accident, I may fear for his life because there is a specific reason that legitimizes that fear.

Now in the case of anxiety I would argue that there are legitimate reasons for this also. You may have anxiety that because of the economy being bad, you will lose your job and be unable to care for your family. To me this is a perfectly legitimate anxiety. You may not have received any official word or even a rumor that your job is ending but because of the specific circumstances around you, taken in total, you have a legitimate concern or anxiety about your financial future.

The type of anxiety that I'm talking about being used for control is much more ethereal and subjective. It is the anxiety that governments, religions and major corporations use to control the sheep, to lure them into a particular religion or to sell them a product or service, to take away their rights.

For example, the perceived threat of Iran developing nuclear weapons. When you hear the talking heads in DC talk about this perceived threat, their statements are full of "may", "possibly", and "could". Nothing specific, no glossy satellite photos of ICBMs sitting on the launch pads, nothing but smoke and mirrors. Much like the propaganda that was rolled out to justify the invasion of a sovereign nation, Iraq.

The continued anxiety methods are used by the government, on all levels, to drive continued erosion of our rights in order to fight the war on Terror, or Drugs, or Poverty. More smoke and mirrors, more hyperbole, more anxiety and the sheeple buy into it gladly giving up their rights (and ours in the process) in the hope of having a degree of security in their own feeble minds.

In the case of religions, most religions use the anxiety of the afterlife and what it may (or may not) contain. The anxiety of mortality and not seeing your loved ones after you die. They play on people's anxiety of their being nothing after death in order to get them into the church doors and pouring money into the collection plate. I am not taking a stance here for, or against, any religion or stating there is nothing after death but illustrating the methods used by most major religions.

Corporations use a wide range of methods either to create anxiety for the sheeple or to play on already existing anxieties. For an example, a few years ago, there was an advertisement on TV where a man was walking around during the course of a routine day but an empty hospital bed was following him. The jest of the advertisement was that even without any symptoms, you could suffer sudden death from a heart attack unless you had one of their cardiac scans. (Perceived) **Problem,** (over) **Reaction**, equals an overpriced, often unnecessary and potentially dangerous **Solution.**

This Problem, Reaction, Solution (PRS) paradigm is used

throughout advertisement and government propaganda to create anxiety for the sheeple. (Essentially the Hegelian dialectic)

Often the anxiety created or played upon is not an anxiety over a physical or even spiritual nature. It can be an anxiety created to fit in or belong to a particular group by buying a product or service. "You have to have an I(whatever) to fit in and be cool" is the underlying message to some of the gadget commercials (don't get me wrong, I do have an mp3 player and enjoy it but I got it because it is a hell of a lot easier to carry when traveling than 100 CDs).

It can be an anxiety over growing old, growing up, growing fat, not growing hair, growing unwanted hair, being disabled, being out of fashion, etc. Some of these anxieties are legitimate to a degree, some of them are created. "You get more respect if you have a full head of hair!" the advertisement cries out! The sheeple sees the ad and thinks, "holy shit! That is why I don't get any respect! My hair has fallen out!" and goes off to buy some drug or have implants done and then is mystified as to why they still don't get respect afterwards. Could it be they were a dickhead without hair and having hair has not changed that? Would never cross their feeble, little sheeple minds.

I think you start becoming a wolf when you start looking beyond the hype to discover what are the true motivations behind what you are seeing and hearing. The problem with perception is that it is subjective and most people don't look any deeper than the audio and/or visual message put in front of them. They don't dig down to see what the motivations are behind the people putting up those images.

Trust nothing at face value. Not what I say, what the TV spews out, not what you read in this forum, not what Thorin writes. Dig deep, study it from all angles, form your own opinion, think for yourself.

Because if you don't, if you let your ideals, opinions and morals are formed, molded, solidified, based on what you read in a book, read on the internet or see on TV without having searched things out for yourself, you are still a sheep regardless of what your t-shirt says.

Are You Free?

A re you free? Think carefully before you answer this one. I'm mainly aiming this towards Americans but anyone can play along. I'll ask again, are you free? I'll even give you the answer…..NO! You are not free. What defines freedom?

Well, let's go back to the good Dictionary and see what this freedom is all about.

"**free·dom** Pronunciation: \'frē-dəm\ Function: noun   1: the quality or state of being free: as **a:** the absence of necessity, coercion, or constraint in choice or action **b:** liberation from slavery or restraint or from the power of another : **INDEPENDENCE c:** the quality or state of being exempt or released usually from something onerous <freedom from care> **d:** **EASE**, **FACILITY** <spoke the language with freedom> **e:** the quality of being frank, open, or outspoken <answered with freedom> **f:** improper familiarity **g:** boldness of conception or execution "The quality or state of being free".

Do you have that? Really? I don't think so. If you live in Amerika, you do not live in a state of being free. You own property, get married, get divorced, work, travel, buy goods and any number of things at the pleasure of the government and only after being taxed for most of the above. Do you own property? Not really. Try not paying property taxes on your land or house and see how quickly the government will take it.

If you are "legally" married, you had to apply for and be issued a marriage license by the government on some level, same with a divorce. When you are born, the government issues a birth certificate and a handy, dandy social security number that stays with you until you die. How about travel? Free to travel you say?

Um, no, sorry. If you are going by car, motorcycle, just about any type of private connivance, you have to have a license, your car has to be tagged, likely has to be inspected, you have to pay taxes on your car, fuel, repairs, tires, brakes, etc. You have to obey the traffic laws, you have to wear your seatbelt, you have to buckle up your child, in some places, you can't smoke in your car if you have a child in the car, you can't talk on the cell phone in most places, you may not be able to park without paying more to some city government agency, you can'…well, you get the idea.

And try getting on a train or ship without ID. Now someone is going to say "you can always bike or walk". Maybe you can unless you look different, then you may get stopped by a police officer and asked for your identification (your papers please comrade). If you are walking at night, it is more likely. You can only cross the street by obeying the laws.

Oh, and the walking shoes or bicycle you are using, you had to pay taxes on. Buying goods? Taxes. Some things, such as prescription drugs, you have to have a prescription for (government mandated), you may have to show ID (liquor, tobacco, some over-the-counter drugs, guns, ammo). Oh, you have to have money to buy goods which calls for a job, which you have to have your Social Security number to get and before you buy goods, taxes are likely already taken out.

Now someone is going to say that you can die without the government's approval or sanction. Well…..no. You can only die the way the government wants you to die. If you die in your sleep, fair enough. Or perhaps in a flaming car accident. OK, guess you don't have to have the government's approval for that (just its approval for the vehicle to have the accident in). But if you are terminally ill, tired of waiting to die and decide to end it all, better do it yourself but the government ain't going to allow anyone to help you without persecuting them and in some states, just attempting yourself is against the law and you can be charged.

And of course, after you die your family has to pay taxes on the casket, funeral plans, etc. A government issued death certificate has to be issued. The government may force an autopsy to be done and, oh yea, I forgot! The fuckers are going to take a huge chunk of what you left behind, if you have much to leave!

Now some fucking moron is going to say "well, if you obey the laws, you remain free". Bullshit! Using that same logic, the women living under Taliban rule were free as long as the obeyed Taliban law. Hell, using that logic, prisoners are free in prison as long as they obey the rules, only go where the warden allows them to go and don't cause trouble.

If you are living on the streets, don't own any property except for what is on your back; you are more free than the, middle-class fucks who mortgage their lives to buy the latest, greatest gadget advertised on TV. The truly poor have a power only equaled by the very rich. Think about that, it is true. The poor have nothing for the government or lawyers to take. The rich can shield themselves from the blood suckers.

Now someone is going to say, "Randal, you aren't free either by your own definition". It is true that I pay taxes and obey the laws (well, most of them), carry ID, etc. But the difference is that I don't delude myself by saying that I'm a "Free American". I fully realize that what freedoms I have left I have at the pleasure of the government. What they can't do, yet, is keep me quiet. They can't take away the free spirit that defines me, they can' shut me up. I can also imagine some stupid son-of-a-bitch saying "If you don't like it, leave!" And my answer is: FUCK OFF! This country was founded by people that saw what was wrong and fought to change it. Our country is 180 degrees away from what our forefathers envisioned for us. We have lost that vision. We have become mired in the consumerism culture. We have become slaves to our own desire to have the latest, greatest gadgets and clothes. Most people in this country don't give a shit who is in power as long as they get to have their mp3 players, cell phones and color TVs. These people disgust me. Don't wave your plastic "Made in China' US flag at me and tell me that I'm un-American. FUCK OFF.

So, my little Sheep enemy, are you free?

The Man At The Helm

Consider the man at the helm of the ship. He is the one responsible for steering the ship through the water, stormy or calm. He may not be the one that picks the route, this may be done by the navigator or the ship's captain but the man at the helm is the one that carefully steers the ship towards the destination picked by the ones responsible for choosing the route. While the man at the helm has a heavy responsibility for following the route chosen and planned, at the end he is usually only following the instructions of others.

Now consider that the man at the helm of the United States is the President and/or the party in power. Using this analogy, this person, or party, is doing nothing more than steering the country towards a destination that has been chosen by others. In this case, let's call these "others" the Powers That Be or PTB.

When you look at the last 100 years USA history it becomes pretty obvious that our country has been carefully steered on a course of becoming dependent on big government and big corporations. The course has carefully been plotted to avoid rocky areas, areas which I equate to personal freedom (personal freedom can be pretty rocky at times and will sink a ship which is being steered on a path of continuous subjugation).

The PTB realized early on that they would never reach their destination in a single journey. It would take slow movement through particularly dangerous areas, stops for resupply and re-charting courses.

As an example, look at the laws that have been put into place since the early 60s. Look at gun laws, restrictions on personal freedoms, taxes and regulations that have developed over the last 50 years and even earlier. Considering that the wolf to sheep (W2S) ratio has changed over the years, the PTB knew that they would never have accomplished their destination by trying to force these things through within a short period of time. The W2S ratio was too heavily weighed on the side of the wolves. The wolves would fight back too much and the PTB ship would crash upon the rocks.

Instead the PTB charted a careful course to avoid the rocky areas and over the course of generations they slowly made the American citizens more and more dependent on the government and dependent on a lifestyle that would turn them into sheep or would produce future generations into sheep that would be easily controlled. Sheep that would readily accept propaganda that generations previous would have been scoffed at by a country largely made up of wolves.

The main political parties are tools of the PTB to keep our country on this course. It makes no difference which party it is, they both have, over the decades, followed this course. What legislation, regulations or taxes one party cannot get pushed through, the other party, once in power, will change a bit and push through. The end result is the same regardless of which party is in power but the sheep believe that because their man or party is in power, that it must be okay.

Layer upon layer, the PTB have slowly buried our country and have done it with the willingness of the sheep which have become the majority in the W2S ratio. The PTB have charted their course well. They have charted the course to come close enough to the rocky areas to scare the sheep into bahing loudly to be steered away from these areas. To the sheep personal freedom is a scary thing. Free thinking has been made to be a bad thing by the PTB because the herd will split if the herd starts thinking freely and when the herd splits, the PTB start to lose control and they just can't have that.

Then once away from the rocky areas, the PTB allow the ship to be steered towards a perfect tropical island and maybe even let the sheep off the ship for a bit of time in order to show them of what can be. To give them a promise of what the PTB can do for the sheep as long as the sheep only give up their freedom and follow the herd. Once the sheep get their taste of freedom, it is back on the ship for their continued journey towards the Utopia that the PTB have promised but which will never be reached. But because the sheep have this vision of this Utopia, they willingly buy into whatever "War on" that the PTB have crafted because the sheep believe that the PTB want this Utopia for the herd and only have the herd's best interest at heart, but nothing could be further from the truth.

Sadly the W2S ratio has shifted over the decades to where the wolves are a very small minority. While the wolves will howl and growl, their howls are lost in the overwhelming cries of the herd that wants to be protected and wishes to reach their destination of Utopia promised by the PTB.

This Utopian vision will never be reached. The sheep may think at times that they are close because their party has been elected or because the sheep has the latest shiny gadget that some movie star has or because some new program has come into place (at tax payers cost) that will protect the herd but this glimpse of Utopia is a carefully crafted vision that the PTB have designed and dangle in front of the sheep and if only the sheep will elect them, or willingly go along with a new law or regulation, this Utopia will be a bit closer than it was before.

Until the sheep stop deluding themselves that our country is the home of the "Free and the brave", stop deluding themselves that the government is there to help them, until the sheep wake up and realize that this illusion is the chains that bind them, our country will never change.

I wish that I was an optimist. I wish that I thought this was possible but I don't. I have been circling the herd for most of my 55 years and have seen nothing more than a continued path towards self destruction for our country. The course may be a bit different or the speed of the journey a bit slower or faster but the destination has not changed.

The USA, as envisioned by the founders of this country, is long gone. The Constitution and Bill of Rights are nothing more than historical documents that were written by wolves for a nation of wolves. The sheep like to think these documents still rule the land but the sheep are wrong.

Because of this I don't buy into the false patriotism that the PTB put up as needed to protect us from our supposed enemies. I won't wear an American flag or wave a "Made in China" US flag on the 4th of July. These symbols still do mean something to me in the context of what our country was supposed to be and perhaps was at one time but not anymore.

I used to get pissed when I would hear someone say that our armed forces were fighting to maintain our way of life because I considered it a lie. Fighting a war in Iraq has nothing to do with protecting freedoms at home but when I thought about "way of life" instead of freedom, I realized this was correct. Our military is not fighting overseas to protect our freedoms but is fighting to protect the "way of life" for the sheep. These wars are being fought to further the course that the PTB charted a long time ago. The "way of life" in the USA is this course, it is this journey.

The sheep think the end of this journey will be Utopia but it won't be. It may appear to be Utopia when it ends but this vision before them will only blind them to the chains that have enslaved them.

A Dying Breed

The term "dying breed" has been applied in several ways. One of my favorite music groups has a song by that title that made me think about if we wolves are a dying breed.

Face it my friends, as a breed, we wolves may be fucked. There will always be a few of us wandering around snapping and snarling at the flock but historically the flock has gotten larger and our numbers have shrunk and continue to shrink until we are so scattered and marginalized that we are totally ineffective.

This goes back centuries; this is not a recent trend.

Past societies, as they got more "civilized" have always become more sheep weighted in the Wolf to Sheep (W2S) equation, always.

Societies love their wolves when they are fighting for survival or to build a new nation. They love their warriors as long as their warriors are fighting to protect the flocks of sheep but once that battle is over, the sheep are scared of the wolves and work to reduce their numbers by evolving their societies to become more sheep friendly. The wolves are kept safely on the edges while the sheep procreate to the point that the W2S ratio has shifted heavily on the side of the sheep.

The sheep further reduce the effectiveness and numbers of the wolves by putting new laws in place that further marginalized the wolves. Laws against freedom push the wolves further from the flock thus making the sheep feel safer. The sheep don't mind the laws restricting freedoms because in their minds, more laws equal more security for the flock. The wolves understand that this is an illusion that more laws make you neither free nor safer but these laws are a security blanket that the sheep don't want to give up.

You see the fewer laws you have, the more you move towards anarchy, the stronger the wolves become and the more their numbers go up. Wolves thrive on freedom. The wolves are happier when they are unrestrained and free to roam and hunt. Free to chase down the weak and destroy them and that is why the sheep are afraid of the wolves.

The sheep are afraid of freedom. With freedom comes personal responsibility and the sheep hate to be responsible for anything. Also sheep don't like wolves because the wolves remind the sheep of what they could be and the sheep don't like thinking that they might be wrong and following the wrong path.

The irony here is that the wolves are a victim of their own success. History's wolves are the ones that founded this country. They were the ones that setup the Constitution and Bill of Rights that gave freedoms to a country that was 90% wolves at that time. But with those freedoms came a prosperous society and thriving economy. Unfortunately it seems that conveniences and a soft life have an evolutionary affect on wolves. As things got easier, future generations of wolves gradually become sheep.

You see it is easier to be a sheep than a wolf. It is much easier to keep your mouth shut and flow along with the flock than it is to stand up and growl. There is comfort in being part of the majority; it gives you a false feeling of being right because, after all, the rest of the flock is going the same way so surely they are right, right?

Barring something like a catastrophic collapse of our society that throws the USA into chaos, the W2S ratio will gradually grow larger in the sheep's favor. Our numbers will grow fewer and fewer. We will retreat further from society and our influence will weaken more so then it is now.

The day may come when the howl of the wolf will only be a memory referenced in some history book but may be put in the context that we were the bad guys.

History is usually written by the victors and in this case, the sheep are winning.

But perhaps I'm being too pessimistic about this. Even warrior societies that are long gone, such as the Spartans, live on in spirit in the hearts of modern day warriors. The soul of the founders of the USA is still alive in a few true patriots. It has not died out completely, yet.

Perhaps the soul of the wolf is deeply buried in some of the sheep, waiting to be kindled into a burning fire that will burn away their wool and reveal the wolf underneath. It may take long periods of adversity for this to happen but much like steel must be exposed to heat to be tempered, perhaps chaos will temper the souls of a few sheep to turn them into wolves.

Only time will tell and while most people hope that our comfortable way of life continues, I'm hoping for chaos. Because only in chaos, only in a collapse of our modern society will the sheep start turning away from the flock and start to realize that the wolves are right in the way we think and live. They will look at the wolves and want to have what the wolves have and the wolves will willingly help the few from the flock that are willing to shed their wool, bare their teeth and follow the pack.

The members of the flock that choose not to follow the hard path of the wolves will perish or live in misery because they have become too fat and comfortable, too locked into the mindset of the flock, to follow the difficult path of the wolves and good riddance to them. Let them be off on their way to their self destruction.

Pursuit Of Happiness

You hear, almost daily, about people not being happy, the pursuit of happiness, comfort foods, being in uncomfortable situations, Ad nauseam.

We have happy hour, happy meals, happy holidays, happy thoughts, and finding our "happy place".

But what does it mean to be happy? What is happiness?

From one online dictionary, we have this definition:

a : a state of well-being and contentment
b : a pleasurable or satisfying experience

What about comfort or being comfortable?

Again from an online dictionary:

a : affording or enjoying contentment and security
b : affording or enjoying physical comfort

or

a : free from vexation or doubt
b : free from stress or tension

When you hear people talk about being happy or being comfortable, it is often used in the context of buying something that will make them happy or having enough money to be comfortable.

But being happy and being comfortable come from within, not without.

Now when I'm talking about physical discomfort, I'm not talking about discomfort related to a medical condition. However, often we have physical discomfort because of the condition we have allowed ourselves to get into.

I am talking primarily about mental and emotional discomfort. And I'm also talking about true happiness, not what the media and corporations tell us we need to have or be to be happy.

How much of what you think you need to be happy is formed by what you see on TV, movies or what your friends or family have? Do you really need that new pickup (which depreciates the second you buy it) or did you friend just buy a new ride and suddenly the 15 year old pickup you had, that was fine before yesterday, isn't good enough?

Do you need a new mongo sized flat panel TV? Isn't the useless shit that comes out of the screen the same from your old 19" as it is from a 60" screen? Or did you see it advertised on TV as being the latest, greatest technology and now you just have to have it to watch useless shit in HD?

If your happiness is dictated from influences outside yourself, you will be no happier than the sheep in front of you that you are following.

If your comfort level is dictated by only being with your own age, race, culture or people in the same economic standard as you are, you are missing a whole world of knowledge and experience.

A large part of being a wolf is being comfortable and happy in almost any circumstances. Keep in mind that "happy" is synonymous with "content". You don't have to be jumping up and down for joy to be happy but just content with your place in life and what you are doing.

Happiness should not be defined by having more "toys" than the next person but because you are a free thinker, make your own decisions, are in good health and physical condition. The things you buy are what you truly need, not what the corporations tell you will make you happy. The corporations put out this continuous line of bullshit and depend on you buying this line. They don't give a flying fuck if you buy yourself into debt, there will be other sheep to take your place when you go bankrupt.

The sheep are "happy" because their lifestyle is dictated by others, by a sort of group think. Their comfort comes by being with others that are essentially carbon copies of themselves.

The wolves are happy or content being by themselves or with their pack. Watching the flock is a form of entertainment for the wolves but while entertaining, it is a puzzling activity they are observing. We are puzzled not because we don't understand what the sheep are doing but because we don't understand the reasons why anyone would want to act that way.

If a wolf finds himself (or herself) amongst the sheep, he will still be comfortable but rest assured, the flock won't be.

Being amongst the flock (but not part of it), may even make the wolf happy since we do seem to get a perverse pleasure from seeing the looks of apprehension, or dare I say fear, in the eyes of the sheep.

Another example between a wolf and a sheep can be seen in churches, political gatherings or social events.

If you put a sheep into a new situation, such as a church different from their own religion, even though he is among other sheep, they are not his flock. Their religious views, political thinking or social standing is not the same as his flock. This may challenge his thinking, force him to explore his own views and he does not like this....at all.

But a wolf in that same situation will be comfortable and open minded. Listening to all viewpoints even the ones that challenge his views. He will either dismiss these as being not for him, modify his views based on new information or actually change his own view 180 degrees since he will find that his way was wrong. The wolves will do this, they will admit when they are wrong and correct their path to the correct direction. The sheep, since they are only following the ass in front of them, wont' change their path except when the flock does.

When it comes to consumerism, the sheep purchase based on advertisements, fads or envy of what someone else has. They will run up credit card bills when the fashion seasons change to buy the latest fashion which covers their asses no better than what they had bought 3 months earlier.

Now don't get me wrong, we wolves also love our gadgets but we buy for need, not want. And when we do buy, we research to make sure we are buying quality. We buy to survive, not to invoke envy from another. You could say that a lot of wolves are minimalist in relation of what their economic status is. For example, a wolf that makes a 6 figure income will have nice stuff but it won't be useless junk that will be obsolete in 6 months like a sheep in the same income bracket. The things that wolves purchase are often of such quality that their family will fight over these things after they are dead.

In the area of comfort, just observe the differences between the wolves in the wild and the sheep in their flocks. The sheep only travel, rest and eat in the same places as the flock does while the wolves will roam, explore, find new things to investigate. The wolves are content to plop down and rest wherever they are, with the pack or not.

So the bottom line here can be found in this quote: "Happiness is the absence of the striving for happiness." - Chuang-Tzu (350 B.C.)

If you have to strive for happiness, sorry to tell you my wooly friend but you will never have true happiness. As long as you allow your happiness be defined by others, you will never be happy. You may think you are happy, but that is nothing more than an illusion of happiness that is being defined by another person or by your flock.

The day you can look around you and be satisfied and content with what you have and who you are, regardless of what society says you should have or be to be happy, that will be true happiness and perhaps you will find that your wool is now a beautiful coat of fur.

Pain In Life

A major difference between the wolves and the sheep is that the wolves understand what pain is, and what it isn't. The wolf will embrace pain and use it to his/her advantage while the sheep will do anything they can to avoid pain.

Now for the purposes of this essay, I'm using pain to describe physical pain and discomfort as well as mental and emotional pain and discomfort. In part because it is just easier to do so but also because to the sheep, any degree of discomfort, physical or otherwise, seems to be painful to them and avoided at all cost.

I believe this avoidance of pain is a major reason why the sheep do not want to leave the flock and why they allow themselves to be led by the sheepherders. To leave the flock or to actually be free and follow their own path would lead to pain, discomfort. As a result, the longer the sheep stay part of the flock, the more they become comfortable with living that kind of life and the less likely they are to leave the flock.

A wolf understands that pain is as much a part of life as pleasure, perhaps more important in fact.

Any woman that has given birth can tell you of the memories of pain while giving birth, but those memories fade as she sees her new child and raises her children to adulthood.

Striving towards a healthy life and physical excellence involves pain, often constant pain. But this pain is, if not forgotten, rewarded when the results are seen in the mirror, compliments are received or the race is won.

Life begins with pain and ends with pain. Trying to live our life's without pain between those two points is foolish and in the end, deprives us of great pleasure and pride.

But often there is no pleasure after the pain and that too is a part of life. I'm not saying here that a cancer patient should not take pain medication to improve their quality of life or that if your leg is broken you should not take the pain pill but my point is that avoiding the pain that comes with everyday living is foolish and something the sheep spend much time trying to do.

Pain is honest and informative. It tells you what is wrong and what you are doing right. It tells you, when exercising, that you are pushing too hard or not hard enough.

Our country went through a painful birth to become independent and free. The founding fathers, willingly, suffered greatly to create this nation. Previous centuries showed a country full of pioneers that suffered, willingly, to open up land, build farms and ranches and create cities. Things like the attempted genocide of the American Indians and slavery aside, you have to recognize their own willingness to suffer pain while also recognizing their faults so we don't repeat them in the future. Embrace what they did right while not repeating the mistakes they made.

But it seems that over the last 4-5 decades, we have transformed from a nation of wolves with a sheep minority to a nation of sheep who strive to avoid pain and discomfort.

As we have become more civilized, we have developed machines to help us avoid pain. We hire people (through the buying of products or support of sports) to do painful things for us.

We have moved from a hunter-gather culture to a culture where the only discomfort we suffer is getting cold in the frozen food aisle of the supermarket.

As a result, our country has grown soft and weak.

A land of sheep who, rather than being free and brave strive to become fat and comfortable.

A nation of sheep who sit on their fat asses watching football and wrestling, eating shitty food and then bitch about how overpaid the athletes are on TV.

A nation of sheep who watch talk shows and cry as other sheep cry on TV about how their childhoods we messed up and how that keeps them from becoming productive members of society.

A nation of sheep who, when they get the sniffles, run off to the drug store for chemicals to "cure" their illness.

A nation of sheep who, after spending all their lives turning themselves into fat sheep, run to the doctor for surgery and pills to cover the symptoms of their poor health that they created.

And our whole society, our corporations and our government has evolved into a massive machine to help us avoid this pain and discomfort.

Our society caters to those that avoid pain by supplying them with "mobility scooters", ramps and automatic doors so they can park their car in the handicapped parking, drag their fat asses into one of these scooters and then drive around the hypermarket buying more shitty food and larger (plus sizes) clothes to encompass their ever expanding bellies.

Now I'm not slamming people with legitimate handicaps here. Some people do have legitimate physical problems beyond their control and things like electronic wheelchairs greatly improve their lives but come on! Go into the big hypermarkets and see who are using these "mobility scooters", a majority of them will be in their 40s or even 30s, double the weight they should be and pulling junk food off the shelves as fast as their pudgy hands can move!

And if you are depressed because your favorite aunt died, you should not have to stand that pain! No sir, we have a pill for you to help you cope with your loss.

If you didn't get hugged enough as a child, we have a disorder just for you! And guess what? That disorder comes with some nifty medicine that will drug you into happiness and comfort!

Our society has become a risk avoidance society where football games are cancelled because it is snowing and the fans might have an accident coming to the game.

A society where peanuts and peanut products are banned in some schools because "little Johnny" might have an allergic reaction.

A society where dodge ball has been banned in most schools because it might cause physical pain and damage self-esteem.

A nation of sheep who avoid pain and discomfort at all cost.

No longer is it "o'er the land of the free and the home of the brave." But now we are the land of the fat and the home of the weak.

But to a wolf, pain is like fire to steel. It tempers the body and mind of the wolf. A wolf will seek out discomfort and pain seeing it as a challenge and a way to become stronger. A wolf, while not wanting his children to suffer, will not try to make their little lives perfect and safe because he knows that through adversity comes strength and he wants his pups to grow up to be strong and free thinking adults

And the greatest pleasures of life will never come to you if you are not willing to put up with the pain and discomfort need to achieve those pleasures.

And to me, there is a difference between pleasure and comfort. Some of the most pleasurable times that I have had were also uncomfortable and/or painful.

This constant striving for comfort and a pain free life is an insidious trap to be avoided.

The more you avoid discomfort and pain, the more you move away from taking risk.

And almost everything wonderful in life involves a degree of risk.

The risk of asking a girl out on a date may lead to a life of marriage, children and love or may end in disaster and divorce but the risk must be taken to reap the possible rewards.

The risk of walking through the door of a new school as a child can bring the reward of a successful career and riches or result in being bullied and broken and living on the streets.

So to any sheep reading this book be warned, it is going to hurt you. It will damage your self-esteem. The words within may be "hurtful", course and obnoxious. This book will shatter the illusions that your flock has been following.

But pain without a goal is futile.

Set your sights on achieving the goal of shedding your wooly coat and taking on the fur of the pack.

Shed the illusion of comfort and peace that you have in your flock and take on the chaos that is free thinking and truth seeking.

Feel the pain and embrace it because only through the pain of learning that everything you thought was right is wrong, will you break free of the flock and join the wolves as we stalk the rest of the flock.

Swatcop

Bullets

✦ I would rather have the respect of an enemy than the pity of a friend.

✦ If a man considers himself a God then he will be crucified by his own words and actions.

✦ You call me a sinner when I confront your lies, I say just call me your personal antichrist.

SwatcopKid

Bullets

✦ One must not lose one's well being in the search for salvation.

✦ You are not a celebrity, you are not what you see on TV, most of you are waiting to be fed by the puppet masters.

✦ I will die on the road to glory and my enemies will pave the way with their blood.

Vance Gatlin II

Ronin

Meet The Pack

I am the one called Ronin, given name Vance Gatlin II. Thank you for picking up this book and looking into our minds and souls, I hope it got the wheels turning in your mind. Thanks to my fellow contributors and Thorin for helping make this happen. Thanks to my beloved fiancée Casey who along with my family supported my efforts. Thanks to my dad, Vance, who taught me that, "Can't never got anything done." Truer words were never spoken. Thanks to the teachers who guided me in school, the soldiers who fight for my freedoms that I will always exercise to insure that their not wasted, and thanks to God for giving me a chance on Earth and I will live to the fullest.

I'm an introvert who has peered deep within my soul and grown stronger and more aware as a result. Forged in the fires of life itself I emerged as my own man. I consider myself a warrior in the battle of life who bows to no man, possessing the inner-strength to face the fires of criticism, and the integrity to never sell out my principles. I view the world with an eye to both sides in search of the truth, giving a basic respect to others, until they show themselves unworthy of that respect. And I realize that only I am accountable for my actions. I will not tread upon, nor allow myself to be treaded upon, what I say, I also do. In the way I see the world I look deep below the surface, questioning everything that I find. My life is my own and the full responsibility of it is the weight I bear willingly.

My goal is to encourage and guide those who read my words to look deeper, think for themselves and become an individual. To see more of my writings, learn more about me, and contact me you can go to my personal website: http://www.roninsjourney. wordpress.com/ or the forum at StalkingtheFlock.com

Reborn

From the moment of my birth
I wasn't my own
Slave to my instincts
Molded by my masters

To be what they thought I should
Not what I thought I could
Mind is racing
Questioning

Mental muscles flexing
Truth and lies that I'm dissecting
Growing stronger
The chains weaker

They watch with growing apprehension
As I begin my ascension
Bonds are loosening
Their fear rising

How can this be
Who is he
As I'm reborn
Bowing to none

Paradox

Nothing but a paradox
You keep trying to fit me in your box
Your worldview is linear
To you I'm just a sinner

Remove your blinders
With them you'll never see the reminders
Of a multitude of thought
To fulfill your mental drought

You see in a two-dimensional view
It is evidenced in the words you spew
Your reflexive horror of differences
Unable to complete sentences

At what you believe is indefinable in me
In reality I define myself as you will see
When you open your eyes and mind
You'll get a glimpse of the views of my kind

Followers of one rule
Think for yourself, so you won't be a tool
Time to shed your wool
Come where for knowledge we drool

To the Badlands
Where ideas are as numerous as the grains of sand
Meet the pack, where debates rage
Join the wolves, as we enter the world's stage

The Shepherd's Warning

Come here little lamb
Sit there by the jamb
I'm going to give your life meaning
And also deliver a warning

From the moment you were bred
You have been led
Get in line
And march in time

Safe from fear
Never shedding a tear
We will protect you
For we know better, too

All we ask is compliance
Punishing those who show defiance
Beware furry demons circle in the murk
Prowling to pull you into the dark

Fear them, for they are dangerous
What they possess is contagious
When they attack, your mental wounds will have an infection
The beginning of an inception

No longer will you be of the flock
Your unused mental faculties will run amok
You'll become what we fear most
One of the rebellious canine foes, as untouchable as a ghost

A wolf

One

One sees tattoos, piercings, and unconventional clothes
One sees the nice person holding the door open for them

One protests because they were told to, and what to say
One protests because they see what's happening and they know
what to say

One quotes the latest news to you
One breaks down the latest news to you

One has a inferiority complex and bluffs strength
One has self-confidence and radiates strength

One sees two "queers" holding hands in the park and is disgusted
One sees a couple on a bench and is indifferent

One eyes the Iraqi behind the counter of the gas station in fear
One questions the Iraqi about his culture

One hears a southern drawl and thinks "Hick"
One hears a conversation about socioeconomic policy

One votes according to family tradition
One votes according to the individual's principles

One sees a muscled-up skinhead
One sees a military veteran

One sees a "heathen" four year old with a Mohawk
One sees four year old standing quietly beside their parents

One sees a single mom, tired and lazy

One sees a single mom, tired and taking online classes while the kids sleep

One sees a racist, fascist pig
One sees a person trying to make the streets safer for their family until proven otherwise

One speaks the party line
One speaks their own mind

One thinks society owes them
One wants society to get out of the way, they got this handled

One is led by their emotions
One is led by their reasoning

One judges a book by its cover
One opens the book and peers inside

One follows the most popular
One forges their own path

One thinks inside the box
One shredded the box and set it on fire because it inhibits them

One has wool
One has fur

One is victim
One is a warrior

One is sheep
One is a wolf

Which one are you?

Bring It!

Have you no respect
Your honor is circumspect
You want me to get in line
When you yourself will not act in kind

Following my online trail
Trying to profile my mind to no avail
Invade my zone
Taking my phone

Where, when, who
Just another monkey in this crazy zoo
Listening in on what I say
For incrimination you pray

Do you know what the Bill of Rights is?
These are the things for which I'll fight
My life you don't have to look inside
I have nothing to hide

I'll look you bastards in the eye
Tell you "Fuck You" with both middle fingers raised high
I'll see you in the Arena of Life
My indomitable spirit will be your strife

The weapons I wield
My logic is my shield
The blade is honesty
My voice will reveal your travesty

Bring it!

The Battle

Welcome to the arena called Life
Gladiators of consequence and circumstance await

No mercy given
No excuse accepted

Do battle or be beaten
Your pleas will not shield you

Your growls will not intimidate
Only the work and effort will aid you

Razor sharp mind
Even then it may not be enough

Do you prefer a slow death of apathy and whining?
The end of your misery I will not give

Watch as I rise to the challenge
Striving for ascension

Dying with a warriors death, with life's head in my grasp
Its body on the floor, no one gets out alive

Battle Weary

Waves and waves of attackers
Pushed forward by the shepherds, their masters
Mounds of corpses piled high
Is the end in sight?

The wolves, the few, strike back
At the whiny little fucks that talk smack
The weak begging for more
Knocking at the shepherd's door

Watching from the distance a warrior shakes his head
Another weak casualty who soul is now dead
Battle scarred and at what cost
The sheep he fights for seem to love being lost

Looking behind him at the battleground
At his brethren who surround
If they knew they could be left alone
They would leave the sheep to rot into bones

Except the shepherds will never stop
So we fight until the last drop
No quarter asked and none given
For those who sold their souls will never be forgiven

Through The Wolf's Eyes

I sit on the hill, watching the masses scurry about.
Dividing and attacking, with their leaders at the helm
The sheep fall and are raised up as martyrs, inspiring others to
rally and join, trying to overwhelm.
Blindly following, as the shepherds continue to shout, demonize,
slander and repeat, their talking points the tips of the swords
they hold to their enemies throats.

Waves of sheep smash against each other and careen to the side,
until I catch the corner of one's eye.
He walks up the hill with a question, "What are you looking at?"
"Look for yourself and answer your own question."
He looks, and sees, and starts to wonder what the meaning is
about.

"Why the conflict? All I see are lambs being led to the slaughter!
Mothers, fathers, sons and daughters!"
"Do you wish to rejoin the fray?" I ask.
"No, I would rather make them pay!"

And pay they shall
When the wolves begin to prowl
Picking off followers
Releasing their shackles

Watching as their hackles rise
And in the eyes of the shepherds, surprise
Their kingdom falls
Trampled by the pack's paws

The end begins
They hear the growls, the sound from Hell's bowels
The pack bellows and howls
Fangs flashing in the light, blood splashing into the night
Freedoms rise and ignorance dies, when the world is perceived
through the wolf's keen eyes

Resist

Gazing overseas, I see attempted revolution
Looking behind me I see nothing but confusion
Over there, the flock is going feral
I shake my head, because this one is sterile

The shepherds' heavy hands
Have been slowly tightening the bands
Draping heavy chains
Until no longer was the flock willing to take the pain

Get in line.
Everything is fine
Do as I say
It will be okay

Hear no evil, see no evil
The population instead began an upheaval
I crack a wolfen grin
Since this defiance isn't a sin

I turn and join my pack
The ones who have my back
We will bite these sheep in the ass
And maybe get some change to come to pass

Ever-Present Rebels

Always circling the flock
The apex predators with their eyes cocked
Facing the meek
Growling at the weak
Ears hearing the commands
Of the shepherd, such a evil man
Formulating strategies to attack
The oncoming wolfpack
The Pack has a variety of methods
Plans to face the shepherds
Some stand in the open and mock
With their middle fingers ready to rock
Using sarcasm to show that hypocrisy runs amok
Other lurk in the shadows
Hidden death without even a growl
On their lips a smirk
As they circle in the foggy murk
Or approach from above on the mountainside
You have nowhere to hide
The growls and howls are our words on living free
From walking through the fires we have gained our Ph.Ds
While victory we may not attain
But we'll go down fighting without shame
Because what's life without a little pain

We're Watching(The Warning)

Moving in the shadows of night
The shepherds work to their delight
Forging subtle chains of enslavement
Your pain is their entertainment

Quietly working
As the lambs are snoring
Careful not to wake
The scattering of rattlesnakes

Pulling their fangs and teeth
So there is no threat to unleash
Chuckling to themselves
Thinking that freedom is shelved

Skirting the edges
Slipping through the hedges
Watching the machinations
As you try for domination

I see you
Know this, I see you
Tremble in your shoes
With me the Wolfpack also stalks

We will not stop
Until you've dropped
So hit your knees and plead
For mercy as we make you bleed

The Beast! The Rage!

The Beast! The Rage!
Clawing out from inside!

Merged with fighting spirit and animal rage!
The warrior with martial fury and razor intellect!

The monstrosity that was released!
Who did it? Who is to blame?!

Do they not realize what they have done!
Unstoppable as time, forged in adversity's fires!

I pity the sheep!
Who released the beast!

The Journey

Padding softly through the streets
Growling at the idiocy that he meets
Searching for truth
Looking through the distortion
Meeting the puppet masters eyes

What was that?
Fear
Untamable and they know it
Unstoppable

The red and black wolf
Walking by mediocrity
Snarling at conformity

Taking the path less traveled
Alone at times
With others at other times
Steady
The wolf

Hypocrisy!

An old man is a perv, an old woman a cougar
Hypocrisy

Bash the ones who call a President the messiah, but raise another up as God
Hypocrisy

Vote yourself a raise, but tell others they make too much
Hypocrisy

Complain about making people show papers, but push for a National I. D
Hypocrisy

Preach conservation and alternate fuels while flying on your private jet
Hypocrisy

Disgust at my tattoos after your boob job
Hypocrisy

False faces with greedy hands, begging for money from the Chinese
Hypocrisy

Flag stamped job outsourcing
Hypocrisy

Scream liar while hiding your own infidelities
Hypocrisy

Claim to be the voice of God while shoving vile sins into the darkness, paying hush money from the pockets of others
Hypocrisy

Hide behind your security all the while trying to take mine
Hypocrisy

Non-profit protecting free speech, but not all speech
Hypocrisy

Suppress one religious symbol while holding up others
Hypocrisy

Tell others their love is wrong, while yours is pure
Hypocrisy

Condemn the Ponzi schemes while running your own
Hypocrisy

Curse the Mosque being built in your city while you send missionaries to their countries
Hypocrisy

Put on a show trial for a company due to its negligence while discarding the fact you approved everything on the rig
Hypocrisy

Bullets

+ I face the shepherd and his flock, the words from my mouth mock, both middle fingers extended and ready to rock. "To be yourself is best, not to be like the rest.

+ I'm disgusted by the lack of spine these days, 'Keep your head down or you'll lose it.' I say 'Fuck that, swing at me and I guarantee I'll make you bleed'. It's better to stand for what you believe, than to live on your knees

+ Talking points are like book titles, easy to remember and not that deep.

+ I don't have a personal library, I have a mental armory of intellectual firepower and my mind is the launching platform

+ Truly believing and thoroughly indoctrinated are only separated by the path taken.

+ If great minds think alike, then explain to me Einstein, Plato, Freud, Galileo, Da Vinci...?

+ Independent thought is hard & liberating, thoughtless acceptance is easy and enslaving

+ A successful debate is one where both parties walk away understanding the other side

+ They say ignorance is bliss , they're wrong it's a fucking bitch

+ Pragmatism rules the day, optimism and pessimism are the lenses that distorts it

Which Are You?

The world has an infection that lies within their minds. I believe most people have an inferiority complex. Here's why, they judge themselves based on others standards, do not trust their own decisions, and follow whatever group they find themselves in. Is this you?

How do you measure your self-worth, appearance, intelligence, etc? Internally, by your own standards, by what makes you comfortable, not to impress? Or by what pop-culture, peer pressure, society dictates?

When making decisions, day-to-day, or big ones, do you listen to the loudest voice, the majority, or whatever your beliefs lay out? Or do you use your reasoning, looking at all sides, weighing the pros and cons, even asking someone who's "been there, done that" successfully for advice?

When meeting people for the very first time, are you completely yourself, confident in your own skin, curious to meet new people but if nothing comes from it, that's fine too? Or do you laugh at jokes that aren't funny to you, agree with everything and try to fit in?

How you answer these questions will tell you where you stand with your true self. Is it a lie, a mask, going with the flow? Or is your action, words, what you see, is what you get? Or do you even know who you are?

The words you have read, or will read in this book, will show you how to not be arrogant, but comfortably confident, not a know-it-all but wise enough to know that you're still learning, to not fit in for the sake of someone liking you, but to be yourself, and drawing people in with your honest self-assessment of yourself. We offer these lessons to you, from a point of experience, insecure, and unsure where we stood in the world, to the self-reliant, confident, and knowing where we stand with OURSELVES individually. It is up to you, to sift through the words, taking what fits, leaving what doesn't. Thinking, questioning and questioning again, the conclusions you draw.

Ascension To Wolf: Defined

Aterm myself, and as you've noticed by now that others use so much of is Wolf. And its opposite number, Sheep. Thorin coined this way back in his first book, "Stalking the Flock." Group-think as opposed to Think for yourself. To limit confusion for anyone unfamiliar with the Wolf Mentality, where it begins and ends, here is a guide. Which are you?

SHEEP: Everything about them is a product of their environment, and the crowds that are popular at the time. Their beliefs are talking points of whichever leaders they follow.

BLACK SHEEP: Start to question and don't accept whatever is told to them. Which can lead to their cliques to start to ostracize them, they question their leaders and the minutes they're criticized, they come to a crossroads. Conform or not to conform. The second they decide to be themselves, they become Wolf, but just a cub at first.

WOLF CUB: This is when you question yourself and look deeper to understand yourself better. You seek to understand the WHY of your particular belief systems. Political, biases, and religion. When you know who and why you are the person you are, and form YOUR opinions, you move to...

JUVENILE WOLF: Then you question everything before you internalize it, not mindlessly accept it, then you are...

WOLF: Full-grown wolf who walks their OWN path, forging their OWN opinions and beliefs with logic, reasoning, and THEIR experiences.

Wolves don't blindly follow but can run in packs of like-minded individuals. But a wolf is still an individual and will not trade their individuality for acceptance. Wolves have friends that accept them, not fair-weather friends. To sum it up, THINK FOR YOURSELF, BE YOURSELF, and BE STRONG ENOUGH TO FACE THE FIRE OF JEALOUS CRITICS

Who Is Your Master/Bow To None

Have you ever asked yourself, "Why did I just do that?", after you acted without thinking? It happens to everyone at one time or the other. Maybe you saw whatever you did on TV before and were subtly trained, and the minute you were in a similar situation you reacted. Reflexively and said/did something that later had you shaking your head. Or seen something where you automatically make a snap-judgment before you even know the details. What made you think that way, something you were told or past experiences? Who is pulling your strings, who is your master?

Your Master; REVEALED!

In the beginning of our lives our master is our basic survival instinct. We eat, fill our diapers, and sleep. Then when we are old enough, our family starts training us. Now they are the master. This usually isn't a bad thing (depending on the parents). But who taught our parents? How do we know they got it right? If members of your family are particularly religious, they may take you to church, synagogue, mosque, mass, temple, etc. More training. Not always bad, though that is a personal decision that you have to make. But how do you know that this religion is right and those are not?

This usually fills the first four years of life, then there's school. So far your masters are parents, and possibly religious leaders. You're young so you don't question that deep yet. Though if adults asked as many questions as kids they wouldn't do foolish things at times. In school, at first is simple, math and English. Facts not opinions. Later, you have science and you learn about how the natural world works; machinery, theories, accepted facts, laws of the universe as humans "interpret" it. But we could be wrong, maybe some discovery that could change everything is around the corner. Humankind is limited by the current technology, so scientific fact can actually be an accepted opinion. Remember, the world was once thought flat and now we have cameras in space taking pictures of the earth, or that the earth is the center of the universe and the sun circles our planet. Now we know we are a little speck in a universe that we can't even see the borders of. Also we learn History but that has parts removed from it, due to space restrictions, ideologies, etc. What's in textbooks is decided by a small group of people and swings between the different ideologies. What is taught is also based on the different schools. I went to a bigger school and then a smaller and found out I was ahead in my class in the smaller school. They hadn't covered the material yet.

Then we have TV and music, another master. Unwed mothers was taboo, then along came a TV show about a pregnant, single businesswoman and brought it to pop culture, homosexuals on TV were taboo and then an actress came out of the closet on TV and real life. Magic was evil, but a book series became a movie franchise that is based out of a school that teaches magic. Good or bad, it's subjective. Don't believe that TV or music has blind followers, I point to people copycatting "famous celebrities". The overrunning of Chihuahuas partially due to the fact that a celebrity had one and maybe even the Mexican food mascot. Music has promoted so much and people jump on the bandwagon and blindly ride it their quest to fit in. The Hippie movement, gangsta thugs and their bling, cookie cutter boy bands, to solo girl singers that sing about the same thing, to just about the same beat. Gossip magazines and TV show you how the "celebs" live, what they wear, drive and do. This isn't bad if you just like to keep up with them due to interest, but when you mimic to be perceived as "cool" and instead look like a fool. And this is just pop culture, a subtle master. Hard to spot its chains.

We also have the Media (TV news, newspaper, and books) which is a more (to me) overt master. What is printed is controlled by an editor, what is on TV is a product of the producers behind the scene. News anchors read TelePrompTers, who writes what they read to us? A subtle word change can affect the whole context of the story. Or pick and choose the stories they think is relevant. If someone is murdered it's one of the top stories, someone defends themselves with a gun, and you rarely see that in the news. TV news hits the highlights; newspapers usually go a little deeper. Books are written by the author's perspective. Some look at an author as a "speaker of the truth" and they have to live their life exactly how the author says and quote them. Because it's the "truth". Not to bash writers, it's all in how you absorb what you read.

Breaking the Chains

So how do you break the chains? Truly believing and thoroughly indoctrinated are only separated by the path taken after all. First you have to recognize the influences in your life. We are shaped by our environment and events in our lives, but is it intelligent design?

That is up to you. Do you blindly follow along and accept everything as, "just the way it is." Or do you question, look for the answers wherever they may be found. Dissect it with a scalpel. Look deeply into it and take what is relevant to you. Not all that is taught to you in life is bad; it's a myriad of facts, opinions, and ideologies. But it is up to YOU to decide what is important in your life.

Parents usually teach you what they think you need to know to prepare you for life. You can go through life with "the plan" and fail miserably because it's wrong for you. But if you analyze and reason, you will see whether it's a good plan, or a bad one. Though to a kid, their parents seem to have ALL the answers, they don't. They do have decades of experiences to draw from and that can be useful to you. In a lot of areas my dad is usually right. I have scoffed, and later learned I should have listened.

Religions teach THEIR worldview, doesn't mean they're right. It is up to you to question, look to other religions, if you're interested. To choose or not choose whichever fits you, not have it chosen for you.

Schools are structured on so many levels, with so many opinions on "what's best for the kids" that you need to independently rationalize in order to identify what is fact and what is indoctrination; you will never know the difference if you don't learn to think about it.

Pop culture is entertaining and can open up minds; I particularly like the ones that have a thought out message. But they are rare and most have cookie cutter songs, movies, endless brain numbing reality TV. Watch and listen with an open mind. Metal doesn't mean you're a Satanist, rap doesn't make you a thug, country doesn't mean you're a backwoods hick. It shows you a different point of view and what you take from it is up to you.

The news media has an agenda. Monetary, ideological, etc., bad news sells, control the information that is shown and it's easier to control thought. One media company is owned by a manufacturing corporation, and every year they have a green week, pushing their products in their news stories. Showing one side of a political issue, and not the other. And when they do show either sides, one shouts over the other or someone gets shorted on time. So look at all sides of an issue, even if you have to hunt it down.

Reborn

From the beginning we are completely dependent and as we grow, what we see, what we are taught, what we hear, and what we experience is added to the matrix of our very essence. The rub comes in how that affects the way you live. A generic product, or customized? Are you just an operating system running a series of programs downloaded directly into your mind? A robot? Or are you the programmer?

As kids our worldview is limited by our environment but our ability to expand our worldview through books, documentaries, the Internet, newspapers enhances or increases our ability to understand it. You can question!

The harder you look, the more likely you will find your answers. Think for yourself by questioning EVERYTHING, and accepting NOTHING blindly. That is the key to being your own master and bowing to none.

Wolf/Sheep Paradox

As a wolf I revel in my uniqueness, and when I was an immature wolf cub I asked myself why I was the way I am. Now I wonder why aren't their more wolves. So many different personalities with so many different experiences. A crowd can see the same thing, but filter it differently due to past experiences and personalities. It makes me wonder if being an individual is easier?

It is less stressful to me; I don't care what others think of me. It's a lot easier to be yourself than trying to fit in and conform. So it seems should there be more wolves. You don't have to even analyze the world, just yourself. But when you make life decisions, it can be hard to find all the data, pros and cons, to make a smart decision. So you can start off being true to yourself, which should be easy. But if you don't carefully think things through, question everything, can you lose the fur? Not if you're a true wolf, we question everything that PERSONALLY affects us, and for intellectual stimulation, even the things that don't. At least in my case that is.

Is it easy to conform?

At a surface level, yes. Take what you hear, parrot it, and go along with the tide. But when you're by yourself, will you feel lost? Who am I? These are rhetorical questions in my case because I have answered them already. But they are important. That's where being a sheep gets hard, possibly, it just occurred to me, why so many people are medicated for depression these days? Just a thought.

If they were honest with themselves, would they be happier?
Is being yourself easy?

Not at first. You have to face the fire of a lot of hard questions about yourself and your influences. That damnable "why" question. It usually opens up so many more questions! But after you have answered these questions, for yourself, now it's easy. Now you have a foundation to build yourself on, now you know WHO you are, your path in life. You don't have to fight the tide like a salmon swimming upstream, or go with it either, because it doesn't matter. You're the rock, just yourself. So in the end, my question was, is it easier to be yourself, or follow along? It's neither, both are hard as hell. But by being true to yourself, you're so much happier. Instead of hating the mask you wear in public.

So why aren't there more wolves? Laziness and lack of inner strength, to lazy to try and to weak because they won't even try.

The Inception Of A Wolf

Curiosity may kill the cat but I question whether or not it makes the Wolf, or at least starts an individual on the path towards being a wolf.

Wolves think for themselves, accepting nothing blindly and questioning everything. Read those last two words again.

Why do we question?

Curiosity. We want to know what, when and why. Everyone has the ability to grow into a wolf. You're born with that curiosity. As a kid you ask questions, now whether you have the initiative to look deeper or stop is up to you.

I'm amazed at some of wolves ages, so young but operating on a mental level beyond a lot of adults. You would think this would be the other way around. Adults have experience after all. So what makes these young wolves a wolf?

The desire to learn, curiosity. They ask the questions, never satisfied, whereas when/if they stop they can get locked in. So curiosity maybe what starts you on the path, but what keeps you there?

Perseverance, initiative. They keep going, asking why. Looking at everything. The second trait. A wolf never stops; they keep going and growing because of their innate curiosity and the ever-changing world feeding it. When you stop questioning, that doesn't mean the world stops and you get left behind in the process.

This is what I see as the starting point for wolves. A trait we are all born with and you see especially in babies and toddlers. They want to learn about everything and get into everything in their process of learning. The key is to never let that curiosity die or you get left behind. The wolf is curious; the sheep only want marching orders.

Awareness

The wolf views the world much differently than most, it maybe the only thing we have in common among all of us. We have awareness; we look beyond what most would view as obvious to find the reason behind different things. A bit like detectives, wolves dig deeper into the context of situations to get to the truth as we see it through honest subjectivity.

This is the reason a wolf isn't a follower. An equal, yes, but not a follower. Wolves don't align themselves with anyone based on superficial wrappings, catchy slogans or traditions. We look past that, look for what is under the public face, the details behind the slogans and "just because that's the way it is" won't cut it. We look at the other sides of the issues, current situations, laws and policies and opposing views. You can have five people witness a car wreck and each one will have a slightly different story. By listening to all of them you can find the common thread and get a more truthful side of what happened. Same method, different situation.

This is why it's hard to fool a wolf. Sales pitches that only tell you the good aspects of a product or people, we look for the downside. See if it has a good balance between the pros and cons. Campaign speeches designed to tap into emotions instead of logic. We can see it from a mile away. A wolf understands that all situations are not one-dimensional; they are instead, three-dimensional, more than just one side to it. That's how we look at the world, and live our lives. Eyes open, ears perked, and minds open. That's the world as seen by a wolf.

STEP UP, Or Get Knocked Down

I've noticed a pervading attitude that is spreading throughout society, or perhaps it was already there and it just now caught my attention. It's a pass-the-buck; nothing is anybody's fault mind-set.

Very convenient for those to weak to admit their mistakes, or to cover the ass of certain members or elements of society. And it helps nothing, and leads towards a decay of society itself, locally, nationally, and globally. And it starts with the individual, and it can be fixed with the individual. Starting with me, and starting with you, my reader.

When events happen, such as mass-shootings, wars, crimes, or public gatherings such as protests; there is always a reaction, emotional or calculating, to disperse blame. On a tool, element of society or individual. All of which is the passing the buck mind-set, a cop-out.

Not even the most persuasive cult leader can make you do something without your willingness to do it in the first place. It's not because you had access to a weapon that you decided to hurt this person. It's not because you heard political rhetoric, or a speech, and that's why you rioted. You didn't strike your wife because of a bad day at work.

It's because you lacked self-control, and the blame lies squarely on you, and your response to life's roll of the dice. A sadly foreign concept in today's world.

First, you have to realize that you have a responsibility to yourself. A personal responsibility, which means that no one is responsible for feeding, clothing, and otherwise taking care of you. Not the government, not a religious institution or charity.

They are not in place to wipe your butt and kiss your forehead and tuck you in. You don't have to be an asset to society, but don't be a drain on it either.

Government programs take money from the producers to enable the societal leeches' habit of irresponsibility and weakness. Charities and churches get donations from altruistic individuals to help those who were dealt a bad hand in the game of life who really need temporary aid. And those who are able and unwilling to work take advantage of this kindness for personal gain from the sweat of others. Thus leaving some truly in need, out in the cold.

This is not to say that you deserve every bad thing that happens to you. Bad things happen, but you are responsible for your reaction to it.

With this personal responsibility comes accountability, where you and you alone, face the consequences of your actions. The triumph of your successes, to the admission of your failings. No book, television show, song, or person is responsible for the actions you take. We all have free will and a mind to filter and reason through the information we take in, though sadly a large part of society seems to not exercise these abilities. And they are still just as accountable for this going along with the crowd decision.

By forcing people to be held accountable and responsible for their lives, they will gain strength or fall to the wayside. Either way, they won't be an ever-present drain on society. When people realize that they alone are responsible for themselves and their families; that food, shelter, water and defense is theirs to provide for themselves, without taking from others directly or through governmental or charitable proxy, then we can make the world a better place. But it all begins with YOU! To quote Thorin, "Excuses are the vises of the weak."

A Political Wolf's Observations

In discussions about politics at work I often confuse whoever I am speaking with if they're unfamiliar with me. They don't see where I'm coming from. Most see the political spectrum as left, moderate, right.

You're a bleeding heart liberal or a greedy heartless conservative. Black and white is how they see the world, and try to fit me in their box. They believe everyone has to be led, and disagree on who should. My rebellious wolf nature, tempered with my pragmatism, confuses them.

I try to explain my views in easy to digest words and seem to confuse them more. I state that I'm a fiscal conservative, social liberal. That means to me that the government runs a balanced budget with a bare minimum of programs and agencies. I also believe in freedom of choice, except I make far less exceptions than a lot of people.

Where I split ways with liberals is where though we agree on freedom of choice, I also believe in personal responsibility for your choices, actions, and words, no safety net social programs for everything. Only for those times where you genuinely hit a stretch of bad luck and need a hand. Where I split with conservatives is that I think outside the box, and tolerate choices I may disagree with.

Perceptions and Power

Many think that conservatives want to force their values on others and that liberals want to tell you how to live because you're too stupid to make your own choices so the government has to do it for you. That's 2-D thinking, look beyond that, think 3-D. The examples I laid out above about the left-right perception has a common theme.

Control.

You've now taken a pure thought and twisted it for your gain. The beginning of tyranny. Those in this realm are my enemies in the battlefield of the minds. They're the shepherds, and those they pander to, and follow them are sheep. It's any way of thinking that forces another's Will on someone that I disagree with, though I allow a few exceptions such as self-defense and justice/vengeance.

Most of society believes someone has to lead, and are perfectly willing to abdicate their authority to someone else whom they've never met. Even those in the middle of the road, the moderates. They like the status quo, sheep that don't bother to think at all or move left and right, up and down, depending on the situation. Moderates can be like black sheep, though this part of the spectrum isn't the exclusive home of that flock.

They question more, not locked in a certain ideology, some thinking that governmental/religious control is needed to keep the extremes in check while willing or not realizing that the chains they're binding others with, entangle them also. While the others are more towards libertarianism. They want both sides to have more freedoms, more tolerant, and more responsibility. Wolves prowl the entirety of the political spectrum, sheep do not. They gather in the areas where some measure of control is present.

Where Do People Fit

You have two extremes, anarchy or totalitarianism. In between these, freedoms are lost, and control is gained. Some believe in freedom of choice, but on various degrees. Pro-choice, you can't tell me what to do with my body, but turn around and say that others have to pay for their healthcare. Some believe that you should have economic freedoms, but you can't marry someone of the same sex. It seems most people have various degrees of self-righteousness.

I noticed a lot of people agree on:

* Freedom of Speech
* No Military Draft (a form of slavery)
* No Corporate Welfare
* Less Taxes and Spending
* No National ID Card

That's more freedom, but they disagree with:

* Gay Rights
* Free Trade
* Letting People be responsible for themselves in old age
* Letting People be responsible for themselves, period
* Legalizing Marijuana

That's less freedom, more control. And a few are undecided on marijuana legalization, corporate bailouts, free trade, and personal responsibility. On two issues they either agreed or disagreed, no maybe, was gay rights and a national ID. This shows me there is a battle for power. Most everyone thinks they know better than you and you shouldn't have the choice. Either for their gain or belief that you should get in line with them. Those I speak with are selfish and/or meek sheep, shepherds/wolves in sheep's clothing, or wolves in wolf's clothing like me.

The former two can't or won't comprehend that I won't bow or get in line. I believe in freedom with responsibility as its counterbalance. Though not an anarchist, I'm not far from it, a minarchist maybe. I realize the need for a structure to protect others from tyrants on personal, business and governmental level. And we are far from that today. This is where I stand, where do you?

A Wolf's Damnation

Society: A History Lesson

In the course of history, societies begin as independent people with a common goal. Wolves usually. But as time progresses, generations down the line, the wolves have been replaced by sheep. How does this happen?

For example, let's look at the USA; we began as an independent group wanting to escape religious tyranny. So we traveled into a largely unknown land with our wits, inner-strength and what we could pack.

No guarantees, you lived or died by your choices. We had more freedom, though still under the Crown, it was harder to reach us. We grew to like this freedom, to rule our own lives, and as the King added more chains to us, the more defiant we became. Until eventually, we politely told the King to "Shove it".

This immediately made us terrorist rebels and we fought against tyranny. Those wolves who led the charge would've surely been tried for treason and executed. If we had lost this war, but we won. Now they're seen as freedom loving patriots, and they took steps to keep this idea alive. To forge a society of wolves.

When laying the foundation for the newborn country, they recognized the Natural Laws. Freedom to speak, to question and protest. The Freedom to defend yourself and have a way to fight subjugation and tyranny should the diplomacy fail. Freedom of your home being yours without trespass. Freedom of privacy, your belongings, papers, yourself and personal space will not be invaded without evidence of wrong-doing backed by oath. A speedy trial in front of a jury of your peers. The prevention of double jeopardy and self incrimination. The recognition that all the natural laws are legal, and that the Constitution limits federal government power.

One caveat though. Since the old wolves that founded this country formed it to be by the people, of the people, who has a government that protects those freedoms and serves us, we had to make sure they did. The Founders designed a system that protected the sheep and let the wolves have room to roam, but the wolves have to be the guardians of the system, a society as free as you could get short of anarchy, or the sheep would ruin it.

The Decay Begins

The foundation is there. But as society grew, popular opinion became laws. Good intentions came at the price of others freedoms and money. Safety nets were built, so your choices weren't as painful, or your choices were made for you in the form of the law of opinion.

To escape this, a few set off again, away from the growing oppressive society. They went west, and eventually as the population grew, it followed. Bringing their rules, and status quo. And again, those who had escaped, them and their kids, were caught in the dumbing down of America. Risk was lessened and cause and affect was numbed. As technology grew, communication went from letters, to telegraph, to telephone, email.

Communication is used to spread ideas and ideas from abroad came over here. It made it easier for those who quest for power to spread their agenda like a virus. To spread the information and propaganda and infect the populace. Before that people relied on themselves, thought for themselves, because if they didn't, the consequence was death. It was harder to corrupt an independent person who used their wits.

These wolves watched and guarded our freedoms. This ability to think, and invent was a double-edged sword that was used against us.

As technology grew, life became more convenient, easier. Not a bad thing as long as you stay sharp, I love my conveniences. I also know how to live without them too.

The reliance on critical thinking was diminished slowly. Group think through the education system helped lower IQs. You're not smart because you can quote Shakespeare, your smart when you absorb it, understand it and discuss it in your own words. When you can apply your knowledge and experience.

Radios were invented, then TVs, Internet, all tools used to spread information quickly. Tools which are used for good and bad, it's the wielder that matters. With the growing mental laziness it became easier and easier to seize control and start people marching to the various leader's beats.

An Opportunity Seized

But it was a product of the populace, with ideas spreading farther and faster, combined with laziness and apathy, the ones pushing the ideas saw an opportunity to implement them. They could play on emotions, encourage greed and selfishness through welfare, and make it where it was expected to be taken care of. Occasions where circumstances created fear, so it was society that stepped in and demanded protection. And seeing this chance to gain more power, the powers of the time acted. And a bit more freedom was lost.

Life is cyclical, and old died and the young rose in power and used these same laws that were left behind to gain even more. Now we have all these little laws telling you how to behave and live. It has become the status quo. Outlawing actions that don't even affect others, such as seatbelts and helmet laws. You can't smoke inside businesses, even if the owner is fine with it. Some foods are labeled bad, others raised up. You can marry this person, but not that one. Whoever is in charge, put there by popular opinion, does your thinking for you. Taking choice away from you. Sheep being led by their shepherds.

Hope On The Horizon?

But scattered among the flock, circling the periphery or even moving away from it, are the wolves. An endangered species now, most every leader, or rich person is a wolf. They used their minds, applied themselves, broke free and rose above. You don't have to be a world leader or rich to be a wolf, you just have to think for yourself. It amazes me how so many put their trust in people they never met.

Some of these wolves are fighting for the return of freedoms, some fight to gain power for themselves, some have just given up, happy to retain their minds, and live within the confines of the sheep world without a whimper. One of my favorite musicians has a lyric that fits it well.

This is true since there is so many of them and so few of us. Is this the fate of all societies to be independent and vibrant at first and then die in apathetic mediocrity until a few cut themselves loose and start anew again, or are hunted down and "re-educated" in a prison or work camp.

The only way to change a society is education, or domination. Present the information and let them choose for themselves, or take that choice from them. Either incrementally (like the U.S now), or all at once (like the U.S.S.R).

We can enter the battle of the minds, for the minds. Or try to live above it all and divorce yourself from society. Or if you're particularly tyrannical, take over. Societies die all the time, the Greeks, Romans, British Empire and now I dare say, the United States.

They begin to decay when independence and freedom goes from people to a centralized point. Then the people are bled dry and the society dies that way, or revolution occurs and the people kill it, and begin anew like a Phoenix rising. So, fight the decay or watch it burn and try again? It's up to you.

VANCE GATLIN II (RONIN)

Predator Or Prey

How do you look at life, as prey, or predator? Do you track it down and seize it or hide from it? What is the difference? Note a predator, any predator, and how they interact with their world. Senses alert, taking in everything, calculating and then risking it with a confident smoothness when they go for the prize.

Now take note of the prey, how they stick to large groups or alone but in sight of another prey animal. They hide from life, let it just happen, live in fear, and generally with no initiative other than their myopic world. Like a squirrel, perched in his tree, munching on his nuts, or you, sitting with your nose in whatever electronic device. And when a threat appears you freeze, and hope it doesn't see you.

How do you approach the world?

Do you sit back like the tiger in the grass, calculating your goals and how to reach them? Alert to everything around you, every possibility. And when you move, its balls to the wall, striving for the prize? Or do you have some like minded friends, working as a team, like a pack of wolves. Effective alone, but deadly efficient together. And when you fail, you learn and try again. Moving forward, but also enjoying life, taking time to relax, but never complacent. That leads to death. This transitions to the "civilized" human world also.

Not physical death, unless you live in a third-world country, but a death of the soul. Blank looks, heads down, shuffling along, locked in a program. Unaware. You can still be aware and be life's prey. By not thinking ahead, living in fear of what's different, what's new. Instead as a new experience, a challenge, as new prey for your predator best.

So the decision is up to you. You can move through the world as an efficient apex predator, taking life by the neck, or gather in a mass hoping nothing bad happens to you. Until eventually you die, never having really lived.

𝔅𝔩𝔦𝔫𝔡𝔢𝔡

Ever notice in some conversations that when you mention something or someone the visual and mental recoiling back like the mere words are poison gas? You mention whichever President and some people would hate them even if they walked on water and healed people. Or the opposite of it, the bowing at the feet of the person, group, or idea. The "can do no wrong" to the "never do anything right" attitudes. Or if they do give credit where it's due, it has a caveat attached to it, "they HAD to do that."

People's egos get in they way of admitting they're wrong, and because of this they fail to grow as critical thinking adults. This also causes problems with personal relationships. Have you ever known anyone who was never wrong? Did you like to talk to them, with the arrogant self-importance leaking from every pore? I don't and have been full of myself where I thought I was right until reality would inevitably come along and give me a Gut check. And if you weren't paying attention, and adjust your point-of-view, then it would happen again. Locked in a cycle, just going around and around.

This is an aspect of the sheep mentality, being taught or seeing only one way, without considering the other. This doesn't allow for all the facts. Whereas the wolves in life take in account everything, and like the sheep, we can be wrong.

What? The Wolf Mentality can be wrong?

Well, no. It's summed up as think for yourself. And that takes in account THAT person's personal experiences, personality, and what they have been taught, researched themselves and what have they tossed to the wayside when filtering this knowledge.

And unless you're omniscient and omnipresent, you don't have the 100% full story. But you do have the information for a more informed opinion.

Without fully examining the actions and motivations of those you love, hate, like or apathetic about, you will remain blinded. Blinded by emotion, with a yoke on your mind, the ability to form a reasoned opinion is non-existent. So instead of holding the world up on a pedestal or under your boot, bring your full focus on the good, the bad, and the why. And then you'll be able to see the world as it is, with 20/20 vision.

Gaining Strength

Since I began studying a Russian martial art in earnest I've heard a phrase quite a bit and want to explore it.

"Don't feel sorry for yourself."

This fits in well with the warrior wolves, and any warrior culture. The phrase may have come from the fact that this is a fighting/survival system used by some of the Russian Special Forces, and whining doesn't cut it in training, or the warrior culture, the Cossacks, that preceded it. Or ANY warrior culture for that matter. Successful warriors don't whine about the odds against them, they overcome them or go down trying. This fits in with the inner-strength that wolves possess.

Self-Pity, we've all have experienced it. I threw a pity party for myself for two years until I realized it accomplishes nothing whatsoever. It causes you to be self-centered instead of looking at the entirety of the situation and the solution. When I realized I was the only one attending the party, I crashed it.

You have a bad day in a broad view of it and you're frustrated and stressed out. And negative emotions are the counter-point to the positive ones; just don't let them control your life. They have a way on feeding on themselves. It's when you have a laser focus on them. These two emotional states are unhealthy, and when you focus on it, the way out is hard to find.

"My life sucks!"

Why? What is the common denominator? Does complaining about it help? Not really, best to focus on the problem at hand.

And deal with it. Life is a series of small battles and curling into the fetal position gets you kicked in the head.

Pity parties lead to stress which leads to grey hair and to a lot of cortisol (stress hormone that help's make you fat, and unhealthy), so instead, except that shit happens, take it in stride, deal with it and keep moving. Calm and relaxed, breathing and enjoying the little things in life, THAT'S what makes it worth living. And you'll be much happier. Otherwise, prepare for hell of YOUR OWN creation.

The War Within

S tudying an ancient Chinese philosopher's book on strategy, I noticed in his thoughts on planning ahead, how those principles can be used in a variety of situations. They work in war, battle, day-to-day, and debate. He lists Moral Law, Heaven, Earth, the Commander and Method and Discipline.

This can be taken as, who is right, environmental conditions, terrain, leadership, technique and the training and foundation needed to implement said techniques and strategies, at least in a fight, on a macro(war) or micro(fight) level. Let's take this stratagem of war into the arena of ideas.

What is Moral Law? Laws foundations are cultural, so look at it on a personal level. What do you believe; your opinions? Have them well thought out before you engage in intellectual battle, because any weaknesses will become apparent. This to a wise wolf isn't a bad thing, because we learn from it.

Environmental conditions, time of day, weather, seasons. On a personal level, well-rested, how you are feeling at the moment, current situation etc. Some are morning people, some are night owls. I know from mid-afternoon to dark, I'm usually drowsy. I'm at my best in the morning and early evening. When you're tired, thinking on your feet is slowed down a bit. Or any feeling of whom you're facing and your confidence levels. It works for and can work against you.

Terrain. Familiar, unfamiliar. Have you thought out the other guy's perspective also, or do you have tunnel vision? Are you in a setting that is comfortable to you? Some thrive in chaos, some look far enough ahead where they function in it, and others are just swept away and defeated. Some like tranquility, like when

I'm sitting on the side of a mountain or walking through a valley. This is where my mind works best, and where others can be uncomfortable. Some like crowds and work well within them; some don't, preferring one-on-one.

The Commander, leadership, what directs your life. So, what does direct your life? Your principles, your personal code. Honor and Integrity or Lies and Deceit. Controlled, well-thought out ideas, with facts as a foundation as opposed to being argumentative with lies and insults. The former is actually very rare in the public arena as evidenced in speeches and debates on TV. Instead of a respect for the other's personal views, instead you find them tearing each other down. This is not how you persuade others, by talking to them like they're the scum of the earth.

Method and Discipline. Your strategy, and how you plan to get there to use it and deal the coup de grace. Do you have the experience and wisdom of how to use it? Have you prepared for any contingency, a counter-point that is unexpected? Is your mind a dull butter knife or a razor-sharp katana in the arena of ideas?

Taking all of these under consideration is how you can prevail in a battle of minds, and the only way it works is critical thought, honest introspection, and the courage to face whatever the answer may be that you face. Which is probably why they're so few leaders of men and wolves, and instead so many shepherds and sheep. Life itself requires a strategy, accounting for all conditions, failings and strengths. At that is the realm that the Wolves dwell, and prosper. Care to join us?

Viking

Know Yourself

The fangs tear at the throat of the sheep before him.
Cutting off the lies spewing forth from this mindless one.
The soft pink skin of lies cover the ugly layer of fat called denial.
Still the wolf tears for what he seeks he knows is there.
There deep down past all the skin and fat is the meat which he
hungers for.
The truth he tears into devouring it all leaving none behind.
This sheep played the part of a wolf for far too long.
As the wolf shows this sheep for its true colors it spews forth more
lies.
The sheep says it can be a wolf given time.
The wolf just looks down and shakes his head.
You will never be one of us for this very reason.
You try to hard to fit in where you think you belong.
The wolf turns and walks away from the helpless sheep.
With one last look at the sheep the wolf departs his last bit of wisdom.
We are not a group or a club to join as you so think.
We know who we are and what we think.
We care not for the masses to like us or to fit to their molds.
So go back and be one with the other sheep.

Throwback

I have been called many names in my life. All have meant nothing to me but one.

That one word was throwback. I still believe in what I was taught by my dad. Say no sir and no ma'am when talking to some one who is older then you. Hold the door for other people if they are coming in behind you. Pick up the phone and call people. Do business face to face when you can. Man up when you are wrong and say I messed up. If you decided to have a child your world ends for you and your world now becomes the child until they are ready to leave the house. Make your word a bond that can not be broken. Have only a few true friends in your life. (A true friend is someone you can call at 0200 and tell them to bring a shovel and all they say is be there in 5). Someone comes at you or yours assume they are trying to kill you and respond in kind. Tell no one that what they think is wrong and let no one tell you that your beliefs are wrong. So I am very happy to be called a throwback.

The End? Or The Beginning? It's Up To You

As you have read this book, you've found that we're an independent and opinionated bunch. Speaking of keeping open minds, and weighing everything before deciding. Standing against that which we disagree with by giving our thoughts and taking the heat. Not doing anything just to go along to get along, while we don't care how you live your life, as long as it doesn't interfere with ours.

You've read essays on how to gain inner-strength and thinking for yourself. How not to quote back our opinions but your own. Quoting back our thoughts doesn't gain our respect, but forming your own, even if it's contrary to our various thoughts, will gain a Wolf's respect.

In a few essays life is compared to war and the views of what's wrong with society as a whole may strike a chord in you. Maybe you think self-reliance and free thought is impossible, or you see how we may have a point. Think about it, think hard, and then decide.

You've seen the easy to remember Bullets, our growls that are our personal opinions distilled into simple but profound lines designed to make you think. The poetry, renegade and howling in defiance, the voices of the various authors taking on so many forms.

Our thoughts, our dreams, in printed word, sharing the knowledge that life has given us, we pass on to you to ponder. Knowing that it runs against the tides of comfort, following others and the latest trends. It's not easy, but nothing worth having is, because then it's not appreciated. And if you question our thoughts, and we don't mind, believe me, By all means contact us, some have websites, emails or you can find us at www.stalkingtheflock.com, register and bring your best game on. We welcome it and not only that, we crave it.